THE GRAPHIC

AN ILLUSTRATED WEEKLY NE...

No. 753.—VOL. XXIX.]
Registered as a Newspaper]
    SATURDAY, MAY 3, ...
    SIXPENCE
    ...ence Halfpenny

EXTERIOR OF LANGENHOE CHURCH

INTERIOR OF LANGENHOE CHURCH

CONGREGATIONAL CHURCH, LION WALK, COLCHESTER
(The dotted portion of the Steeple was shaken down)

IN THE HYTHE, COLCHESTER : THE RUSH FOR THE GASWORKS

PELDON CHURCH

ROSE INN, PELDON

ON THE QUAY, WIVENHOE

COTTAGE AT ABBERTON

THE RECENT DISASTROUS EARTHQUAKE IN EAST ESSEX

Extract from *The Graphic*, showing destruction in the Colchester area following the 1884 Essex earthquake. (Reproduced by courtesy of the Essex Record Office.)

ESSEX EVENTS

Death, Disaster, War and Weather

The fire at Little Chesterford in April 1914 that destroyed two farms, eight cottages and two public houses.

ESSEX EVENTS

Death, Disaster, War and Weather

IAN
YEARSLEY

Phillimore

1999

Published by
PHILLIMORE & CO. LTD.
Shopwyke Manor Barn, Chichester, West Sussex

ISBN 1 86077 101 7

Printed and bound in Great Britain by
BIDDLES LTD.
Guildford, Surrey

This book is dedicated to Kevin and Alison, who have shared some of the most momentous events in my life.

Contents

List of Illustrations

Frontispiece: The fire at Little Chesterford, April 1914.

Acknowledgements

The illustrations in this book are reproduced by courtesy of the following: Brightlingsea Museum/ Alf Wakeling, 121; Cater Museum (Billericay), 30; Derek Barber, 146-7; Derek Chapman, 87, 102, 161; Colchester Museums, 45, 51; Essex Chronicle Series Ltd., 33, 41; Essex Police Museum, 32, 34, 36, 42; Essex Record Office, 5, 8, 28, 47, 49, 52-3, 55, 78, 89, 101, 109, 118, 125; Essex Record Office/Essex Police Museum, 74-5, 110-1, 128; Essex Record Office/John McCann, 88; Essex Record Office/Shiner & Holmes, 71-3; LCGB Ken Nunn Collection, 114, 116-7; National Maritime Museum London, 119-120; Southend Borough Council/Essex Record Office, 107; Southend Pier Museum Foundation, 103-4; Cyril Taylor, 97; The Trustees of the Imperial War Museum, London, 13-15, 22, 25. All other pictures are from the author's collection.

The author would also like to thank the following for their help with the research for this book: Barnado's; Braintree District Council; Brightlingsea Museum/Alf Wakeling; Cater Museum/C.E. Wright; Chelmsford Cathedral; Chelmsford Library; Chelmsford Museums Service; Coggeshall Heritage Centre/Douglas Judd; Colchester Museums; Corporation of London; Epping Forest Museum; Essex Chronicle Series Ltd.; *Essex Countryside*; Essex Police Museum/Fred Feather/Elizabeth Farnhill; Essex Record Office (Chelmsford & Southend Branches); Great Dunmow & District Historical & Literary Society/Rev. Peter Street; Great Dunmow Town Council; *Halstead Gazette*; Harwich Maritime Museum/P.L. Gates; Hedingham Heritage Group/ Charles Bird; Barbara Howe; Imperial War Museum; Kathleen Jones; Kelvedon Museum/Julian Hardy; *Leigh Times*; Locomotive Club of Great Britain; London Borough of Barking & Dagenham; London Borough of Havering; London Borough of Redbridge; London Southend Airport; Maldon District Museum Association/Len Barrell; Mersea Museum; National Maritime Museum, London; National Motor Museum (Beaulieu); National Railway Museum; Andrew Phillips; Southend Library; Southend Museums Service/Ken Crowe; Southend Pier Museum Foundation/Peggy Dowie; Staff at Witham railway station.

Introduction

This book about Essex events has to be selective. The county has a long and interesting history and a full account of everything that has happened would require several volumes.

The idea for this book arose from the author's study of the county's early photographic history—in particular, the pre-First World War era of the popular postcard. A picture paints a thousand words and many of the illustrations in this book have been selected as much for their dramatic impact as for the tale they have to tell.

The audacity of some of the early postcard publishers recorded in these pages is at times overwhelming. Who today would dare to issue a set of postcards of a train crash in which 10 people died? Or to publish a picture of a fire in which half a village was destroyed? Such intrusive coverage today would only be featured in less reputable tabloid newspapers. Someone in the future may well wonder how even the tabloids dared to show such things.

Yet such pictures retain a certain fascination, as if satisfying some sense of morbid curiosity. We look at photographs of rail crashes and wonder how anyone survived them. We look at pictures of flooded houses, in awe at the terrible forces of nature. We look at pictures of war victims, in horror at the terrifying destructive forces of Man.

This book is divided into themes. It begins with war, as no story of Essex events would be complete without warfare, from the earliest battles with spears to the modern air-wars of the 20th century. The 1648 Siege of Colchester and the aerial bombardment of Essex towns in the Second World War are among many remembered conflicts.

Criminal activities, too, are included, from the sensational 'Moat Farm Murder' in Clavering in 1899 to the horrific murder of PC George Gutteridge at Stapleford Abbotts in 1927.

It covers the great Essex Earthquake of 1884—not the first Essex earthquake, but certainly the first to be captured on camera. It looks at the history of flooding in Essex—a constant threat to this low-lying,

coastal county—most graphically illustrated in recent times by the horrifying 'Great Tide' of 1953. It looks at storms—and, of course, the 1987 'hurricane' is there. It looks at ice and snow—usually carried suddenly to this east-facing county from the frozen wastes of Siberia—and remembers such incidents as the disruption caused by the severe winters of 1947 and 1963. It looks at fires, ranging from the Wilson's Corner fire in Brentwood, which claimed a well-known department store, to the 1914 'village fire' at Little Chesterford which claimed almost half the village's houses.

A section on transport includes early road accidents, such as the day in 1913 when a tram toppled over in a gale at Barking. The much-photographed Cromer Express disaster at Witham in 1905 is featured, as is the Colchester rail disaster of 1913. Shipwrecks, too, are covered—a maritime county such as Essex has suffered many of them over the years. More recent have been air disasters, ranging from early balloon flights to modern jets.

Not all Essex events, however, have been unpleasant. This book also features light-hearted sections, from the visit of the Home and Atlantic Fleets to Southend-on-Sea in 1909 to the celebrations of VE Day in 1945. There are also bizarre and unusual events, such as the wager to see if 'seven Hundred men' could fit into a waistcoat and the discovery of a witch skeleton in a remote coastal town.

We are fortunate, as we look back with characteristic, modern-day nostalgia, that many events which took place before our own lifetimes have been recorded for us on camera by far-sighted individuals who photographed incidents that otherwise could not be imagined. These photographs, supplemented by engravings, sketches and vivid news-reporting, help us to understand what it was like to witness some of the events that made Essex history.

The county and its people have witnessed many wonderful and varied events over the centuries. This book provides a selection of those that hit the headlines.

CHAPTER I

War

Essex has always featured prominently in wars between Britain and other countries.

The oldest known offensive weapon, a broken wooden spear dating to before 200,000 B.C., was found at Clacton-on-Sea in 1911. When Boudicca (Boadicea) destroyed the Roman settlement at Camulodunum (Colchester) in the first century A.D. she was following in the footsteps of a long line of wartime combatants.

There are several major dates for warfare in Essex places:

991: the Battle of Maldon, a bloody encounter between the defending Saxons and invading Vikings at Northey Island in the River Blackwater near Maldon. The Vikings made a series of raids along the coast and landed at Northey intending to attack Maldon by crossing the causeway linking the island to the mainland at low tide. Local people were alerted to the attack and called for reinforcements under the well-known and highly respected Saxon leader, Earldorman Byrthnoth.

Byrthnoth arrived before the tide had gone out and exchanged insults with the Vikings across the

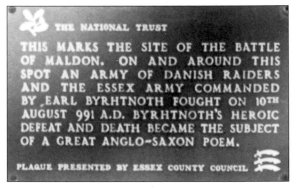

2   The plaque commemorating the Battle of Maldon on fields next to the river near Northey Island.

narrow strip of water separating them from the mainland. As the waters receded, the Vikings tried to cross the causeway, but were repeatedly driven back. They then asked to be allowed to cross the causeway and have a fair fight on the mainland. Incredibly, Byrthnoth agreed! The outcome after this gentlemanly act was surely predictable—the Saxons were defeated and Byrthnoth killed.

1   The causeway to Northey Island from the mainland over which the Vikings came to fight the Battle of Maldon in 991.

1

The Battle of Maldon is commemorated in an epic poem, apparently written by an eyewitness to the event, and also by a modern embroidery, commissioned in 1991 to mark the one thousandth anniversary of the battle.

3 The site of the Battle of Ashingdon (1016), looking from Ashingdon Hill to Canewdon Hill, the camps of the Saxons and Danes respectively.

1016: the Battle of Ashingdon was another Saxon-Dane confrontation. The English King, Edmund Ironside, gathered his troops on Ashingdon Hill near Rochford faced by the Danes, under Canute, on Canewdon Hill opposite. The battle was fought on the plains between the two hills where, thanks largely to a defection by one of Edmund's allies, Canute was victorious and the English were defeated. Four years later the Danish king ordered a church to be built at Ashingdon in memory of those who had died in the battle.

Medieval warfare was more sophisticated and led to a spate of castle building as various noblemen fought to protect their interests. Significant castles or castle buildings survive for example at Colchester, Hadleigh, Hedingham, Pleshey and Stansted Mountfitchet. Most saw little active warfare, though Colchester and Hedingham both had to endure sieges.

In summer 1648 the Civil War involved Essex in one of the most significant episodes of the whole campaign. The Royalist army, led by Sir Charles Lucas and Sir George Lisle, took refuge in the old walled town of Colchester where they waited for

4 A modern photograph of the church at Ashingdon, built by King Canute in 1020 to commemorate the dead of the Battle of Ashingdon four years earlier.

5   The shooting of Sir Charles Lucas and Sir George Lisle in August 1648 following the surrender of the Royalist army at Colchester during the Civil War. A monument in the grounds of Colchester Castle today marks the spot.

reinforcements against the pursuing Parliamentarian army led by Sir Thomas Fairfax. A siege quickly developed; the Royalists were trapped in the strongly fortified town—much to the annoyance of Colchester people—and the Parliamentarians erected a ring of forts to prevent the Royalists from coming out for supplies and reinforcements.

Inside the walls conditions deteriorated as food ran out and the besieged were reduced to eating horses and dogs. Two of the town's churches (St Mary-at-the-Walls and Greenstead) were damaged by cannonfire, as was the ancient priory church of St Botolph, now little more than a ruin. After two months inside the town, when food supplies and ammunition were exhausted, the Royalists surrendered. Their leaders, Lucas and Lisle, were taken to the castle and shot.

After the Restoration of the monarchy, the Dutch were the enemy, and in 1667 made an audacious manoeuvre up the River Thames, attacking Canvey Island and firing shots at the tower of East Tilbury church. The tower was destroyed and has never been completely rebuilt.

In the late 18th/early 19th centuries the serious threat of invasion by Napoleon led to the construction of a chain of protective forts around

the south and east coasts of Britain. Many of these forts—known as 'Martello Towers' after a legendarily strong structure at Mortella in Corsica—still survive.

The south coast towers were built first; the east coast towers, including those in Essex, were constructed *c.*1809-15; at the end of this period Napoleon was defeated at Waterloo and the threat of invasion was removed.

The towers, however, were called into action during several subsequent conflicts when invasion was expected, most recently during the early years

6   The ruined tower (left) of East Tilbury church, destroyed by the Dutch in 1667.

7 One of a chain of Martello towers which was constructed around the south and east coasts of England in the early 19th century to protect the country from an expected Napoleonic invasion. Eleven Martello towers were built in Essex—this one stands to the south-west of Clacton.

of the Second World War. They were used then as observation posts, billets for the Home Guard and mountings for anti-aircraft guns.

Several Essex towns also built barracks to help with the defence of the county. Colchester, Shoeburyness and Warley all had sizeable establishments and men left from there to serve abroad in South Africa in the Boer War of 1899-1902.

In the 20th century, many more Essex men fought—and died—in the trenches of the First World War, whilst for the civilians at home there were airborne attacks, principally by Zeppelin.

At the start of the First World War in 1914 Germany's Zeppelin airships were one of the most potent weapons available to either side. Zeppelins (and other similar airships) had been used extensively for civilian purposes in Germany in the pre-war years and, with air warfare in its infancy and aeroplanes used primarily for reconnaissance purposes, they were expected to figure significantly in its outcome.

8 A rare photograph from 1902 of a parade at Epping to mark the return of troops from the Boer War—a campaign which involved many Essex men.

Zeppelins were not sent to Britain until the early months of 1915—when they were used for high altitude night raids—and they wrought little damage on the country's war effort. Nevertheless, the hum of the engines and the sudden appearance of bombs, indiscriminately dropped from the darkness, greatly frightened the civilian population, who might glimpse the big, slow-moving fleets of Zeppelins in the moonlight overhead. Germany's airship raids lasted until towards the end of 1917 when the warning systems and defence aircraft were improved.

One of the worst-hit Essex towns during the First World War was Southend-on-Sea, which suffered several Zeppelin raids. In May 1915 there were two major attacks on the town, the first taking place on 10 May. Ten of the 11 rooms at the Cromwell Boarding Establishment in London Road were gutted by fire. Houses were damaged in Baxter Avenue and West Road in Prittlewell. A serious fire also occurred at Flaxman's timber yard in Southchurch Road. One person was killed in the attack—the prominent Salvation Army member, Mrs. Whitwell, who was asleep in her bed at North Road, Prittlewell, when the bombs were dropped.

Bombs also fell over parts of Leigh, Southchurch and Westcliff, whilst the now-vanished Southend Technical College suffered a near-miss when a bomb embedded itself outside in the roadway.

9 1915 saw several Zeppelin attacks on Essex, including almost certainly this one at Coggeshall (attributed by the postcard's publisher to an aeroplane) where a bomb landed in a field belonging to a house called Starling Leeze. After the war the site was bought for £1,200 by public subscription and a memorial to the town's 78 war dead was placed—according to local tradition—on the exact spot where the bomb had fallen. The field and the memorial are now part of the town's recreation ground. The soldiers standing around the crater are thought to be members of the Warwick Regiment, which was stationed at Coggeshall during the war. The town of Colchester was also hit on the same night.

10 Spital Road, Maldon, after a night of Zeppelin activity on Friday, 16 April 1915. An airship approached the town from the river and hovered over the workhouse before dropping at least 20 explosive and incendiary bombs. Numbers 21 and 25 Spital Road were badly damaged, whilst surrounding properties, including many in nearby Mount Pleasant, suffered shrapnel damage to windows and tiles. A bomb crater also appeared in a nearby meadow. The white weather-boarded cottage in the picture is still there, as is the tall building in the left background.

11   Wrecked House in London Road, Southend-on-Sea, 1915.

Two pictures from 10 May 1915, showing the results of a Zeppelin attack on what the Germans described as the 'fortified town' of Southend-on-Sea. The Cromwell Boarding Establishment in London Road and the private house in Baxter Avenue were two of several places hit during the May raid, the first of two major night attacks in the area that month.

12   German Air Raid in Baxter Avenue, Southend-on-Sea, 1915.

13   Zeppelin crash—wreckage, Great Burstead, 1916.   14   Zeppelin crash—wreckage, Great Burstead, 1916.

Two photographs of the wreckage of Zeppelin L32 at Great Burstead, one of two German airships brought down over Essex on the night of 23/24 September 1916.

According to eyewitnesses, the enemy airship hovered over the town for about 30 minutes using a searchlight to pick out targets such as the electricity station and the railway line. There was no response from anti-aircraft guns—a particular point of annoyance in the post-attack discussions. Hundreds of people ran into the streets to see what was going on. Cartoons in the local paper offered the latest 'iron suit' for air-raid protection.

150 bombs were dropped in attacks on southeast Essex on 10 May and £6,000 worth of property was destroyed. People in Southend were incensed by the attack on their town and organised a riot against German shops, during which several windows were broken and property damaged. The local newspaper, the *Southend & Westcliff Graphic*, was equally aggressive in its editorial, commenting that 'the person with German blood in him is rightly considered to be a dangerous enemy ... "Once a German, always a German" is absolutely true. A clean sweep is the only remedy'.

An anti-English message was dropped from one of the Zeppelins, stating that the attackers would 'kill or cure' the population. The *Graphic* responded, professing that 'people who converse in German in English streets have something to hide'. The newspaper was unflinchingly scathing about the attack, reporting with sarcasm that 'nearly 30 bombs were dropped at Leigh and doubtless the Iron Cross will be awarded for a [pet] thrush that was killed'.

The second raid, a fortnight later, claimed two more victims—a seven-year-old girl in Broadway Market, Southend, and a female visitor to Southbourne Grove in Westcliff who was killed by falling shrapnel from an anti-aircraft gun. Leigh, Westcliff and Southchurch were also badly hit, and outlying villages such as Great Stambridge suffered from aerial destruction.

By 1916, however, Britain's air defences were beginning to cope with Zeppelin attacks. In March, Zeppelin L15 was shot down over Southend and crashed into the River Thames. Six months later,

15 An aerial shot of the fired wreck of Zeppelin L33 at Little Wigborough. Note the security cordon to keep away souvenir hunters.

the first Zeppelin to crash on English soil landed just over the Essex border at Cuffley in Hertfordshire, shot down by the airman William Leefe Robinson on 3 September 1916. Three weeks later, on the night of Saturday/Sunday 23/24 September, two more Zeppelins were brought down, this time in Essex.

The first (L32) was shot down by a plane over Billericay and crashed in flames in a field in the parish of Great Burstead. The second (L33) was hit by anti-aircraft fire from London defences and, losing height through lack of gas, crash-landed at Little Wigborough (on the northern shore of the River Blackwater). Both were of a new design and were a serious loss to the German forces.

The *Essex Chronicle*, careful not to reveal exact locations, referred to them only as happening in 'southern Essex' and 'on the Essex coast' (respectively), but local people knew exactly where the airships had landed and thousands visited on Sunday morning to see for themselves what the airships looked like and to claim souvenirs of balloon material and metal frame.

The Billericay Zeppelin came down in a field to the east of Greens Farm Lane (formerly Jacksons Lane), where surrounding hills 'provided natural balconies … for spectators' so that the whole event

'looked like a gigantic bit of stage management'. Watchers in Billericay High Street saw the flaming airship pass over the town and hundreds of people followed it to its final resting place, where it impaled itself on an oak tree—that classic symbol of the British countryside—the tree being 'battered and burned, but still upstanding and alive'. The flames from the airship were so intense that it was possible to read a newspaper by their light. The crew, all of whom were killed, were buried at Great Burstead, but were later removed to a national German War Graves Cemetery.

As the first batch of sightseers watched the burning mass of L32 at Billericay, they saw another light in the sky, indicating that a second airship had been hit. The fate of L33 was different as its gas balloon had only been ruptured, and the crew tried to flee for home across the North Sea. However, they did not have enough fuel left to make the journey and they turned back over the Blackwater, looking for somewhere to land.

They chose some fields at Little Wigborough, where the airship eventually touched down in a 'textbook landing', straddling the road from the village to the church. The crew got out and set fire to the airship before knocking on the door of a nearby cottage to ask the way to Colchester,

16 A memory sketch of Zeppelin L33 at Little Wigborough.

where one of them had apparently worked before the war. The cottage's occupants were too scared to answer the door and the Germans set off up the road towards the village without getting any answer. They were eventually taken into custody by the local policeman and were transferred by soldiers to the village hall at West Mersea for the night. A crowd assembled outside and gave three cheers for the King! The prisoners were later taken to Colchester barracks.

Like the Billericay crash, the Wigborough Zeppelin also attracted a large crowd—even at 4am, not three hours after the airship had landed, the roads around the village were blocked with horses and carts, bicycles, pedestrians and army vehicles, as people came from all over the place to see what was going on. Some even arrived by aeroplane!

Despite being fired, enough of the Wigborough airship survived for spectators to see its bulk for themselves—it was said by one eyewitness to look like the 'skeleton of a prehistoric beast left stranded by the sea'. Money collected from visitors was donated to the Red Cross and other war charities.

Numerous items ejected from the airship during the crew's vain attempts to maintain height were found in the surrounding countryside, including guns, maps, bits of machinery and even food. Part of the

Zeppelin can still be seen—along with several newspaper cuttings about the event—in Little Wigborough church.

The destruction of the two airships was wildly celebrated. The *Essex Chronicle* led with the headline 'Illuminated Essex Resounds With Cheers' and followed it up with the observation that 'never was there such a day as Sunday for sightseeing'.

1916 was also memorable locally for another event, in which the Essex-based Great Eastern Railway (G.E.R.) steamship captain, Charles Fryatt, was murdered by the Germans in retaliation for ramming one of their submarines. Fryatt was master of the steamship *Brussels*, which had crossed the Channel

17 Part of the wreckage of Zeppelin L33 at Little Wigborough—now on display in the parish church.

despite the close attentions of German submarines. During a second crossing after the ramming, the Germans were waiting for him and he was captured and shot. The event, however, caused outrage in England and the Germans suffered badly in the propaganda war. Fryatt's body was returned to Essex and buried in Dovercourt churchyard, where a memorial to him was erected by the G.E.R.

In 1917 Southend was again under aerial attack, this time by aeroplanes—Gotha bombers—which caused much more damage than the Zeppelins and more deaths. The town was heavily involved throughout the war; prison ships for British-based German civilians took their charges on board at the end of the pier and for a time the *Palace Hotel* was used as Queen Mary's Naval Hospital.

As the First World War progressed, Essex people became involved in several special 'Weeks': 'Aeroplane Week', 'Warship Week', etc. At Chelmsford, a biplane on display in front of the Shire Hall proved a real attraction to publicise these events.

When the aerial bombardment ceased at the end of the war, the sea yielded something else of interest. The surrender of the German U-Boat submarine fleet was overseen by the Harwich Naval Force, led by Commodore (later Admiral, Sir) Reginald Tyrwhitt, which escorted over 150 submarines to the historic Essex port. The submarines were anchored three and four abreast between Parkeston

18 A memorial to Captain Charles Fryatt, master of the G.E.R. steamship *Brussels*, who was murdered by the Germans in 1916 after he used his ship to ram one of their submarines. The memorial, in Dovercourt churchyard, was erected by the G.E.R. 'as an expression of their admiration of his gallantry'.

19 An unusual photograph of a bi-plane outside the steps of the Shire Hall in Chelmsford during Aeroplane Week, *c.*1917. Aeroplane Week—a rallying call for donations to pay for new aircraft—ran from 5-11 May and the publicity included posters carrying slogans such as 'I can go up to 15,000 feet—Can you go up to 15 shillings?'.

20 Surrender of the German Fleet, Harwich, 1918.

SURRENDER OF GERMAN FLEET
BRITISH NAVAL OFFICER TAKING OVER
SUBMARINE FROM GERMAN OFFICER

GERMAN U-BOAT OFF HARWICH.

21 U-boats at Harwich following German surrender in November 1918.

The caption of the first picture is not quite correct—the German High Seas Fleet was taken to Scapa Flow; only the submarine flotillas (and one or two smaller vessels) were taken to Harwich. The second picture shows one of the larger long-range U-Boats.

22 Wreckage of the German plane which crashed at Clacton-on-Sea on 30 April 1940, showing soldiers guarding some of the scattered wreckage.

14

Quay and the Suffolk village of Shotley on the other side of the River Stour.

At the outbreak of the Second World War, Essex was again caught up in enemy activities. Following significant advancement in aircraft design and capabilities since 1918, the aerial war was to become much more of a feature than it had been during the First World War. In the early months of the conflict, Essex coastal areas in particular came quickly under attack.

Southend Pier was commandeered for military use to become the major control point for shipping in the Thames Estuary. Harwich was again important as a port, no more so than when HMS *Gypsy* was destroyed within sight of the town by floating mines dropped from German aircraft in November 1939.

Such was the activity around the county's coastline that Essex inevitably claimed the first civilian casualties on the British mainland, when, on the night of 30 April 1940, a low-flying German bomber lost its bearings and crashed into houses at Victoria Road, Clacton-on-Sea, killing two residents and injuring 150 others. Over 500 properties in Victoria Road, Skelmersdale Road and Albert Gardens were damaged. Air-raid precautions were swiftly put into practice and soon several wardens were on the scene.

The plane, whose four crew members also died, was carrying two bombs, only one of which exploded on impact. The unexploded bomb was not discovered at first; some used it as a temporary seat

before they realised what it was! It was later taken away for examination and defusing.

At the retreat from Dunkirk in late May and early June 1940, hundreds of Essex men and vessels joined the 'Little Ships' armada to rescue soldiers trapped on the beaches as the Germans closed in. It became one of the most talked-about operations of the war and saved thousands of lives.

By June 1940, the skies above Essex were filled with aircraft, both hostile and friendly, night after night and, soon, day after day as well. Essex airfields were particularly important for the defenders and were major targets for invading aircraft. Searchlights, gun sites and radar stations around the county also played their part in defence, particularly during the Battle of Britain.

As 1940 wore on, there were more and more attacks and more and more buildings suffered from

23 A seat at the junction of Victoria Road and Albert Gardens in Clacton-on-Sea commemorating the German bomber crash of April 1940. Claiming the first civilian lives lost to enemy action on English soil, this was a landmark for both Essex and the aerial campaigns of the Second World War—hence the importance of a local memorial.

24 Most, but not all, of the 'Little Ships' made it home safely from the Dunkirk rescues of 1940. This memorial in St Clement's churchyard in Leigh-on-Sea—a traditional maritime community—pays tribute to all those who went to Dunkirk and remembers especially the crew of the *Renown*, who never made it back.

25 The remains of a German bomber shot down over Chelmsford in June 1940. The house in the trees on the right was the home of the Bishop of Chelmsford.

aerial bombardment. In the last months of the year three Essex churches, which had survived for centuries, were damaged or destroyed.

On 16 September 1940 the church of St Peter-ad-Vincula at Coggeshall was undermined by a bomb which landed in the churchyard by the north-west corner of the tower and went down at an angle 25 feet beneath the building. The roof of the nave collapsed, dragging down the north arcading and the roof of the north aisle. The tower was so badly damaged that it had to be taken down and rebuilt—it took until the early 1950s before it was restored and in use again.

Today the church displays photographs showing the damage done and the work during restoration.

Five days after the Coggeshall church bombing, an even worse fate befell the parish church at Little Horkesley. A new weapon, a parachute mine, was dropped on the night of 21 September 1940 and scored a direct hit on the church. Rare, centuries-old wooden effigies and brasses were seriously damaged and the building itself was completely razed to the ground. The local public house, the *Beehive*, was also destroyed on the same night. The only other 'community' building in the village, the old schoolroom, was soon doubling as both pub and church!

26 The display in the church of St Peter-ad-Vincula at Coggeshall, commemorating the damage caused to the building during the Second World War.

27 Photographs and landmine shrapnel in Little Horkesley church, demolished by enemy action in September 1940 and rebuilt in the 1950s.

The foundation stone for the new church was laid in 1957 and the building, designed to reflect the style of the old one, was consecrated the following year. A famous local poem was written about the night of 21 September; it is on display in the church, together with photographs of the damage and a fragment of a parachute mine which fell in the area.

On 13 December 1940 a third Essex church was hit. The building at Stock was badly damaged when a landmine fell in the churchyard. Windows were blown in and the nave roof lost most of its tiles. The rectory, the Congregational Church and numerous other buildings in the village also suffered blast damage from the explosion. Weddings were held in the belfry while the church was undergoing repair. In 1953 a garden of rest and remembrance was created in the churchyard on the spot where the landmine fell.

Aerial bombardment continued to the end of 1940 and the casualties grew. On 13 October the Mayor of Chelmsford, John Thompson, was killed in an air raid, with his wife (and Mayoress), Emma, and several members of their family.

The war progressed and the tide began to turn in favour of the Allies. In Essex there was a new

28   The parish church at Stock following German bombing in December 1940.

development. From 1942 onwards American forces began to arrive in the county, to build airbases and to fly from Essex soil. Many of these airbases can still be seen and memorials to those who flew from them are spread around the county.

In 1944 a new weapon was launched against Britain—the V1 'revenge weapon', commonly known as the 'doodlebug'. The V1 and the later V2 were terror weapons which claimed many lives in the latter part of the war. Conventional bombing still had a part to play, however, and there were moments when this too brought much fear and destruction, even as late as the last 18 months of the war.

On 22 February 1944, for example, St Botolph's Corner in Colchester was seriously damaged by a massive incendiary raid, which caused vast disruption and devastation.

Another propaganda success for German bombing took place on 19 December 1944 when the Hoffman's ball-bearing factory at Chelmsford—makers of parts for aircraft engines and other war machinery—took a direct hit. Neighbouring roads also suffered. 29 factory workers and 11 local residents were killed. A 'ball-bearing' memorial to Hoffman's

staff who were killed during the war is in Chelmsford Cathedral, where it was placed when the factory closed in 1989.

By the end of 1944 the end of the war was in sight. Essex people could already contemplate nights when they could sleep peacefully in their beds and the days when they could walk safely in the streets.

They played their part throughout the Second World War, as they had done for centuries in defending the county against enemy aggression. They manned ports, anti-aircraft guns and ARP stations and built aircraft, ships and all manner of machine components in local factories. Airfields such as Debden, North Weald and Hornchurch were never busier. Shipyards at places like Wivenhoe, Brightlingsea and Wallasea Island built countless vessels. The River Thames at Southend and the harbour at Harwich were filled with ships and soldiers. Everyone in the county was contributing to the war effort.

The wars of the Romans, the Saxons, the Vikings, Napoleon and Hitler have all left their mark on the history and geography of Essex. One can only hope that they are the last.

CHAPTER II

Crime

Before the Essex police force was set up in 1840, the responsibility for law and order in the county rested with parish constables, local magistrates and even farmers. The Peasants' Revolt of 1381 and the 19th-century agricultural riots pre-dated full-time policing, whilst the fighting navvies of the railway companies arrived on the scene around the same time as the law-enforcement officers.

From the early 19th century some significant criminal cases have made the headlines in Essex. One was the murder case at Berden in March 1814.

The parish constable and local shoemaker at Berden was a man called Henry Trigg, who lived with his parents in his shoemaker's shop. On the night of 25 March 1814, two burglars entered the shop to steal some leather. Henry was awakened by them and went to warn his elderly father before going into the shop to tackle the men.

A struggle ensued between Henry and one of the intruders and they both fell to the floor. Henry's father then joined the fray and helped his son pin the man to the ground. The other burglar immediately produced a gun and fired a warning shot above their heads. They jumped to their feet, but, with a cry of 'I'll do for you!', the gunman

29 The leaning gravestone of Henry Trigg in Berden churchyard. Trigg, a parish constable and shoemaker, was murdered by two villains in March 1814.

fired another shot straight at Henry—and he was killed on the spot.

The burglars left in a hurry, forgetting a hat, a lanthorn and two sacks of leather which they had bagged up for stealing. It took some time to track down the men responsible, but the hunt eventually led to William Pratt and Thomas Turner, two persistent offenders who had carried out several other burglaries on the Essex-Hertfordshire border.

While under arrest at Chelmsford jail, Turner cracked and admitted that the two men had entered the Triggs' premises with the intention of stealing leather and that he had been grappling on the ground with Henry whilst Pratt had fired the fatal shot. Pratt was then questioned and also admitted involvement, but insisted that Turner had been the gunman. The jury at their trial in March 1815 found both men guilty of murder and they were hanged shortly afterwards. Henry Trigg was buried in Berden churchyard. His worn, leaning gravestone is now the only physical reminder of that fateful night in the village shoemaker's shop.

One of the most sensational 19th-century Essex crimes was the murder at Doddinghurst of 20-year-old Jael Denny by her lover Thomas Drory. The event, in October

30 A classic illustration of the murder of Jael Denny at Doddinghurst in 1850. This picture was also used, however, to illustrate other similar 'crimes of passion' of the Victorian period, even in cases where strangulation was not involved!

1850, was a classic 'crime of passion' of the Victorian era.

Jael, with her mother and stepfather, had been living at the Drory family home as servants and 23-year-old Thomas Drory had taken a liking to the younger Jael. They were often seen about together and, as the newspapers would report, were on very intimate terms.

A few weeks before the murder, Jael and her parents moved out of the Drorys' home, Brick House Farm, to a cottage near Comber's Farm, a couple of fields away. Thomas and Jael were on such intimate terms that she became pregnant and Jael—and her parents—obviously thought Thomas would marry her and set up home together. Drory had other ideas.

When Jael was seven months pregnant, her mother chastised Drory about rumours that he was planning to become engaged to a certain Miss Giblin. Where, she asked, was his respect for her daughter, who was carrying his child? Drory became uneasy about the whole affair and started his own

rumours that Jael intended to take her own life. He also forced her to write out a note, apparently in return for payment, stating that he wasn't the father of her baby, though everyone knew that he was.

As the day of birth drew near, Drory became ever more agitated and, with over eight months of the pregnancy gone, he arranged to meet Jael in the fields one evening for a supposedly romantic interlude. It was the last time Jael was seen alive.

The facts did not become clear until early the following morning, when Jael's mother and step-father, alarmed at her failure to return, set out to search the surrounding fields, believing that she might have fallen into a ditch and drowned. They found the poor girl's body face down in a field, with a rope around her neck.

As Thomas Drory was the last person known to have seen her alive, he was collected by the police and taken to the murder scene to view the body. He was reluctant to approach as they drew near to the site and suspicions immediately began to fall upon him. A rope which matched the one used in the murder was later found in his house and he was soon arrested and charged. He was quickly found guilty and was hanged the following year.

The funeral of Jael Denny was a sorrowful affair. Her family was very poor and 'a one-horse hearse of the commonest description received the pauper coffin' as the body was taken to Doddinghurst parish church for the funeral service and burial. It was interred 'in a retired corner of the churchyard', which did not stop large numbers of morbid souvenir hunters from visiting the grave and taking away pieces of turf from the site of the murder.

Another horrific crime, from November 1850, was the murder of PC Robert Bamborough at nearby Hutton. Bamborough had been assigned the task of taking a convicted poacher, William Wood, from Billericay to Brentwood, where the prisoner would be collected for onward transmission to Chelmsford jail. The two men were handcuffed together for the journey, but the road was long and in places remote and there was plenty of opportunity for a convicted criminal to try to get away.

Wood saw his chance as they reached Church Lane in Hutton. He began to struggle with the officer and the two men fell into a pond. As they struggled in the water, Wood forced handful after handful of foul-smelling mud into Bamborough's mouth and eyes and repeatedly hit the officer around the head with his handcuffs. He then managed to free himself as PC Bamborough lay spluttering in the water and escaped in the direction of Church Lane.

Before he had gone a few paces, however, he stopped, retraced his steps and lifted the officer's head out of the water, before turning around again and rushing off down Church Lane. Two young witnesses saw the event and it was this last act of compassion that ultimately saved Wood's life.

PC Bamborough was removed to the *Chequers* public house for medical attention, but was too badly

31 A memorial to PC Robert Bamborough, marking the site of his murder in Hutton in November 1850. The memorial was unveiled in 1990 during the commemoration of the 150th anniversary of the founding of Essex Police.

injured to recover and died nine days later on 30 November 1850. Wood himself was caught at Chatham and charged with murder. The evidence relating to his lifting the officer's head out of the water spared him from the gallows and he was instead convicted of manslaughter and transported for life.

Another conviction for manslaughter was secured in the so-called 'Tolleshunt Knights Case' of April 1884. Drinking partners, Thomas Smith and Aaron Beckwith, left the *Plough* inn in Oxley Hill after a seemingly quiet night of discussion when they suddenly started to fight each other in the road outside, apparently over a girl. Smith produced a knife, stabbed Beckwith in the groin and pushed him into a ditch, leaving him there before heading off home.

The following morning, Smith was on his way to work when he found Beckwith crawling along the road. The latter implored Smith to get some assistance and Dr. Salter was called from nearby Tolleshunt D'Arcy. Despite medical attention, Beckwith died the following day. He was buried at Tolleshunt Knights parish church. Smith fled to Colchester but was arrested later at Tiptree. He was very repentant at his trial and there was a general belief that the two men had been equally responsible for the fight.

The following year another police officer was murdered. Inspector Thomas Simmons and a colleague, PC Alfred Marden, on night-time patrol in January 1885 had seen three men acting suspiciously at Romford, and Marden had been posted as observer while Simmons went to investigate. They had already recognised one of the three as a known burglar, David Dredge, so there was good reason for their suspicion.

As Simmons approached the three men to ask what they were up to, the tallest of the three shot him without warning. They then scattered across nearby fields, with Marden in pursuit—until he was shot at himself. Simmons was fatally wounded by the first bullet and died four days later.

THE

WAKES COLNE TRAGEDY.

PORTRAIT OF THE MURDERED WOMAN.

Below we give a report of the trial of George Sargeant, the Wakes Colne murderer. The prisoner was sentenced to death, as there was every probability from the first that he would be. The sentence will in all likelihood be put into execution on Monday, the 13th of August. We are now able to present to our readers a portrait of the woman who was so brutally murdered. The picture, which is a very faithful one, having been carefully engraved for us from a good photograph, shows that the deceased had a comely appearance. She was only 21 years of age.

He appeared much dejected and covered his face with his hands to conceal it from the curious gaze of the on-lookers. Upon arrival at the Prison he had to bid farewell for ever to his own clothes and assumed the convict's garb, which he will now wear until his end.

VISIT OF HIS PARENTS.

The prisoner's father and mother, a humble couple getting on in years, who live at Sudbury, visited him at the Prison on Wednesday afternoon, a few hours after his trial. Prior to doing so, Mr. Sargeant called at the shop of a tradesman in Chelmsford and purchased an old sack in which to take away his son's private clothes. He entered into conversation with the assistants at the shop about the murder, and said of course he could not make any sufficient excuse for the crime which his son had committed, but believed it was a fact that the deceased had not treated his son well and had caused him a good deal of irritation.

A PROBABLE PETITION.

In some minds there seems to be considerable dissatisfaction that the case should not have been fully tried. People seem to think, that the Judge would have done well not to take the accused's plea of " guilty," or at any rate, not before he had been made fully aware of the consequences of the plea and the difference between manslaughter and wilful murder. It is said that a petition will be got up in which this fact will be recited, and an endeavour will be made to prove that the accused must have been out of his mind at the time he committed the deed. Taking into consideration the fact that the condemned man has suffered from a sunstroke, and had been drinking prior to the deed, the petitioners think it may be inferred that his mind was most probably unhinged for the time being.

THE KNIFE FOUND.

During the week diligent search was made for the knife with which the murder was committed, some scores of people, besides the police, looking in vain for it in the barley field in which the prisoner said he threw it. On Monday afternoon, however, about three o'clock, P.c. Mower, of Bures Hamlet, who was accompanied by Constables Bird, Pratley, and Wade, caught his foot against something hard, and stooping down, he found a double-bladed clasp knife, with a buckhorn handle, both blades shut, and rusty, apparently, from blood. The larger of the two blades is about three inches in length. This, it is believed, is the instrument which caused the poor woman's death, although, probably, it cannot be traced directly to the prisoner's possession. It was picked up within about two yards of the footpath, and one end was buried in the earth, as if it had been trodden upon.

ANNIE SARGEANT, THE MURDERED WOMAN.

THE SCENE OF THE MURDER.

The scene of the murder is called the Lane Farm, a pretty little homestead, abutting on the Colne Valley Railway at Wakes Colne. It is divided into two tenements, one being occupied by the family of the murdered woman, and the other by a family named Bull, one or two

32 James Lee, one of three men involved in the murder of Inspector Thomas Simmons at Romford in January 1885. He was ultimately hanged for his part in the tragedy.

33 Press coverage of the 'Wakes Colne Tragedy' of July 1888. George Sargeant stabbed his wife Annie to death in front of their baby daughter.

David Dredge was arrested in February and detained for questioning. His tall colleague, James Lee, was subsequently arrested in London when he tried to pawn the murder weapon, but the third man, for the moment, eluded capture.

The trial of Lee and Dredge was somewhat controversial, as both men believed they would not be given a fair trial. Their case, however, went to court, and Lee was found guilty of murder and subsequently hanged at Chelmsford jail. Dredge was found not guilty of Inspector Simmons' murder, but had to face another case of the attempted murder of the pursuing PC Marden. His alibi for not shooting Inspector Simmons is said to have been that he was 'shooting at PC Marden elsewhere at the time'! The third man, James (or John) Martin, was later arrested for the murder of a policeman in the north of England and was tried and hanged at Carlisle.

Three years later the 'Wakes Colne Tragedy' made newspaper headlines around the county. The event took place on 17 July 1888 when 21-year-old Annie Sargeant was stabbed by her husband George during a domestic dispute at Lane Farm farmhouse near the Colne Valley Railway.

Sargeant, an army reserve man, labourer and former railway employee, had gone to visit his wife at her parents' house, 'whither she had flown with her baby for protection' after he had become drunk and started behaving aggressively towards her. The discussion soon degenerated into violence, as Sargeant pushed his wife to the floor, produced a knife and stabbed her behind the ear, before 'kicking her about the head like a savage'.

The incident was witnessed by Annie's mother, sister and child and Sargeant was visibly shaken immediately after the murder when his sister-in-law held up the baby and shouted, 'There, look at your

34 Sergeant Adam Eves, who was killed by a gang of corn-stealers at Purleigh in April 1893.

IN MEMORIAM
SERGEANT ADAM JOHN EVES
ESSEX CONSTABULARY
WHO WAS MURDERED WHILE IN
THE EXECUTION OF HIS DUTY
15TH APRIL 1893
AGED 36 YEARS.

THIS TABLET IS ERECTED BY THE
WHOLE OF HIS BROTHER OFFICERS OF
ALL RANKS AS A MARK OF ESTEEM AND
REGARD FOR HIS BRAVERY.

35 The grave of Sergeant Eves in Purleigh churchyard. 163 police officers and 10 ex-members of the force attended his funeral.

wicked father!'. He later said 'I hope she [his wife] will go to Heaven; I know I shall go to Hell'. The *Essex Chronicle* was aghast at the whole incident, reporting that 'a more sickening scene has never occurred in the whole history of crime'.

Sargeant was hanged in August on the evidence of his own admission. Annie Sargeant was buried at Wakes Colne parish church on Sunday, 22 July, amid incredible scenes of hysteria as hundreds of sightseers came by train to the village to witness the funeral and view the house where the deed had been done.

Sightseers were a bane to many criminal inquiries in the late 19th and early 20th centuries, including one at Purleigh five years after the Wakes Colne village murder.

On the evening of Saturday, 15 April 1893 Sergeant Adam Eves was on his way home from delivering a note to the *Royal Oak* pub on his round at Hazeleigh when he encountered a gang of men stealing grain from a farm at Purleigh. Without warning, they attacked him mercilessly, clubbing him to death, slitting his throat and leaving him dead in a ditch by the roadside. The body was not discovered until the following day, when a huge murder enquiry was immediately launched. Word soon got round and hundreds of people turned up in the village to view the murder scene and collect souvenirs of hedge cuttings and unrecovered grain.

Clues from the case soon led to a number of local men and six arrests were made. Maldon police station and courthouse, where the prisoners were taken, also attracted large crowds. Two of the prisoners, Richard and John Davis, previously convicted poachers and thieves, were found guilty of the murder and sentenced to be hanged.

The following year another Essex case attracted widespread public interest. On 25 June 1894 the body of a young local woman was found in Prittle Brook, not far from the village of Prittlewell in the south east of the county. The deceased had been shot in the head and there was blood from the wound on the path and grass nearby. Crop marks in an adjacent field showed evidence that her assailant had probably lain down in wait for her as she passed by.

The victim of the crime was Miss Florence Dennis, an intimate acquaintance of a London Docks clerk called James Canham Read. In a case that bore similarities to the Jael Denny murder, Florence was pregnant with Read's baby and had recently discovered, much to her horror, that he was already married. The two had been seen together on Sunday, 24 June, the day before the discovery of Florence's body, and suspicion immediately fell on Read.

36 James Canham Read, protagonist in the 'Prittlewell Murder' of 1894. He killed his pregnant girlfriend, Florence Dennis, and dumped her body in Prittle Brook.

Up until then, Read had been considered a man of good character—'sober, educated, intelligent'—but he arrived suspiciously late for work on the Monday, having missed his train back from Southend. When the dead girl's sister rang him, before the body's discovery, to ask if he knew of Florence's whereabouts, he denied all knowledge of having seen her and then immediately vanished, taking with him a sum of money from his firm.

As investigations developed, it became apparent that Read, though married and outwardly respectable, had had a series of liaisons with other women. The web of deceit had finally closed upon him at Prittlewell and he was eventually tracked down to an address in South London and arrested.

A huge crowd gathered to see the suspect when he arrived at Southend for questioning, just as they had done at the murder scene. This interest reached its peak as Read was charged with Florence's murder and, after a long and widely reported trial, was ultimately found guilty and hanged at Chelmsford. Florence was buried at St John's church, Southend.

One of the most sensational murder cases in Essex history was also one of the earliest to be properly photographed. The Moat Farm Murder—at Moat Farm (formerly Coldham's Farm) in Clavering captured public imagination and led to the production of a series of images of the murder scene, the farm and, of course, the murderer himself.

The affair began in 1899 when Samuel Herbert Dougall and a rich middle-aged spinster called Miss Camille Holland moved to Moat Farm planning to settle down together as a couple. Within a few weeks of their move, however, Dougall tried to seduce a young servant girl, Florence Havies, who told Miss Holland about the incident. Shortly afterwards, on

37 Moat Farm, location of the infamous murder of Miss Camille Holland by Samuel Herbert Dougall in May 1899.

38 Another view of Moat Farm. Photographs of the building became very popular when the facts of the murder there came to light in 1903, four years after the event.

19 May 1899, after an argument about the attempted seduction, Dougall and Miss Holland went out for a trip together. Miss Holland never returned. Dougall told Florence that she had gone to London and that he would be picking her up from the station later that day. Florence later testified that Dougall had subsequently left the house several times, but had always returned alone.

The following day Florence ended her employment with the couple and left with her mother for work elsewhere. A succession of girls—including a hitherto unknown wife of Dougall's—came and went over the next few months and relatives thought that Miss Holland had simply become reclusive and was too embarrassed to reply to their letters. Bankers and stockbrokers still continued to write to her, however, and they still kept getting replies …

This strange situation continued uneventfully for four years until the local police officer heard gossip about Dougall's suspected unlawful activities. Discreet enquiries were made into his financial affairs and it became apparent that some of Miss Holland's documents contained forged signatures.

Dougall was arrested for forgery and a search of Moat Farm for Miss Holland began. Walls, floors and even the moat were checked. After extensive searches, her body was discovered in a covered ditch which a farmworker recalled he had been asked by Dougall to fill in shortly after her disappearance.

39 Some of the thousands of sightseers who visited Moat Farm during the murder trial in 1903 to see the place where Miss Holland's body was found (the cross in the foreground marks the spot). The sender of the postcard from which this picture was taken was evidently amongst their number for he or she writes: 'I have just been to see Miss H.'s grave'.

40 Dougall under arrest at Audley End station.

Though badly decomposed, the body was easily identified as that of Miss Holland, largely on the grounds of the exceptionally small and rare shoes that she was wearing, and Dougall was convicted of her murder and hanged at Chelmsford prison on 14 July 1903. The *Essex Chronicle*, reflecting the strong support for capital punishment of the time, recorded that 'the awful history of Dougall shows him to have been a terrible miscreant, dangerous to society, and the world is well rid of him'.

Another sensational case from the early years of the 20th century was the so-called 'Basildon Murder'—the double-murder of an elderly couple in Honeypot Lane, Basildon. The couple, Mr. and Mrs. Watson, were collecting water from a pond on a neighbour's land early one morning in August 1906 when they were encountered by the land-owner's two sons, Richard and Robert Buckenham (or Buckham), aged 20 and 17 respectively. Richard, in particular, took exception to the Watsons' activities as he wanted to use the pond to water his cows. He asked them to stop taking water and they refused, so he shot them! He then went to their house—a two-roomed bungalow—and robbed them of a watch and some money. The boys were

quickly tracked down, arrested and taken to Billericay police station.

The case attracted a lot of interest. The murder scene itself was visited by thousands of people—'by train, in motor cars, on motor cycles, in carriages, brakes, wagonettes, on cycles, and even on crutches'! People cut branches from the trees round the pool to take as souvenirs.

When the case came to court it was equally popular. 'Quite a number of Basildon residents waited outside the court for some time before the hour for beginning business,' reported the local newspaper. 'As soon as the doors were opened to the public there was a rush for the vacant places and every inch of room was speedily filled.' The boys, not surprisingly, were found guilty.

In the years leading up to the First World War a new 'crime' phenomenon reached Essex streets, as suffragettes—women dedicated to getting for women the right to vote—chained themselves to buildings and deliberately damaged property. Several incidents took place in Essex, including a report from the vicar of Braintree that his church had to be kept locked to prevent suffragettes from entering and damaging it.

DOUBLE MURDER

NEAR BILLERICAY.

HUSBAND AND WIFE SHOT.

TWO BROTHERS ARRESTED

CONFESSIONS BY BOTH.

PATHETIC SCENES AT THE FUNERAL OF THE VICTIMS.

A terrible double tragedy came to light at Basildon, near Billericay, on Thursday, the 23rd of August, the dead bodies of Albert Watson, forty-seven, and his wife, fifty, being found lying at the side of a pond off Honeypot-lane. The couple had occupied a bungalow in the neighbourhood, which is a remote one. Watson had a gunshot wound in his right loin, while Mrs. Watson had a similar wound in her chest and on her left arm. The wounds are dreadful to behold, and suggest one shot at the man and two at the woman. Four fingers may be placed in the wound in the woman's breast.

At seven o'clock on Friday morning two young men were arrested on a charge of murder.

The accused are Richard Buckham, aged 20, and Robert Charles Buckham, aged 17. They are brothers, and are described as labourers. They live with their father at his house on the land where the bodies were found. The two young men were charged with the murder, arrested, and conveyed to Billericay Police-station on Friday morning. In the evening they appeared before Mr. A. Ward, J.P., at Billericay for a formal remand.

Both are slimly built. The elder is dark. The younger was much affected, and cried. Police-Supt. Marden deposed to the arrest of the prisoners, and produced a double-barrelled gun, from which it was supposed three shots had been fired, and which, he said, had been found in the house occupied by the prisoners.

The Superintendent then asked for a remand until Monday, which was granted.

STARTLING CONFESSIONS BY THE ACCUSED.

PRISONERS WEEP IN COURT.

The two accused young men were brought up on remand before the Billericay justices at the local Court-house on Monday, and charged with the wilful murder of the dead couple. Quite a number of Basildon residents waited outside the court for some time before the hour for beginning business. As soon as the doors were opened to the public there was a rush for the vacant places, and every inch of room was speedily filled.

The justices present were:—A Ward (in the chair) and E. T. Mashiter, Esqrs., and Lieut.-Col. Kemble. Supt. Marden conducted the case for the prosecution, which was also watched by the Chief Constable of Essex, Capt. E. M. Showers.

Previous to the hearing the mother and elder sister of the accused visited the cells in which the prisoners had been located since their arrest, and the meeting was very pathetic. Both mother and sister cried bitterly as they left the Police-station and walked down the street.

barrelled breech-loading gun (produced) and as he did so, Richard said

"That is what I done it with."

I examined the gun and found both barrels charged with the two loaded cartridges produced. I conveyed the prisoner Richard to Billericay Police-station, and Sergt. Giggins conveyed the prisoner Robert in a separate vehicle. At the station I again cautioned them, and charged them as before. Richard said, voluntarily,

"I wish to tell the whole truth for mother's sake. I did go into Mr. Watson's house and took 4s. 8½d. and a silver watch."

Robert said,

"He showed me the money and watch when he came out, but I did not have any of it."

Supt. Marden added: My depositions are not complete, but that is as far as I can go to-day.

The elder prisoner, when asked if he wished to question the Superintendent, began to make a statement, but the Clerk advised him to make no statement then.

Supt. Marden said he was instructed to say that the Treasury would take up the prosecution, and to ask for a remand until next Monday.

The Chairman (to the accused): You will be remanded in custody until this day week.

Supt. Marden: Take them back.

The prisoners were then removed to the cells, and later to Chelmsford Prison, where they arrived shortly before three o'clock.

having saved a little money, he came to this district about six months ago to spend the rest of his days quietly in the country. His wife and he lived under the happiest conditions, and were sober and respectable people, regular attendants at the Basildon Mission Chapel. They have two sons, one an architect in Canada and the other a sailor on H.M.S. Victory. The couple occupied a bungalow, containing two rooms, with a small shed at the back. It is in a wild district, about five miles from Billericay, and from three to four miles from Pitsea. The nearest houses are about a quarter of a mile off. The man was found in a very small pond which had been dug out some time ago to provide water for the cattle. His wife lay near by on the clay. The man was face downwards, in about 18 inches of water. They were within a few feet of one another.

Mr. and Mrs. Buckham came from the neighbourhood of Bromley-by-Bow about two years ago to the brick bungalow occupied by them, but, while poultry and stock are kept in the country, Mr. Buckham still follows his old profession as an engineer, proceeding to Old Ford, London, daily by the early morning train from Laindon station, and returning in the evening. In this family there are two sons (the prisoners) and four daughters, one of the last-named grown up. The family are naturally much distressed at the sad position of affairs. Mr. Buckham, before he had any idea that his sons were to be arrested, was considerably affected by the fact that the tragedy had occurred on his property.

THE HOME OF THE WATSONS.

INTERVIEWS WITH THE ELDER PRISONER.

A resident of the neighbourhood passing the dismal pool by which the tragedy was enacted on the evening after the discovery found the elder prisoner, Richard Buckham, there alone, and got into conversation with him. It was just before dusk. The two spoke of the dreadful affair, and remarked upon the blood which was still visible on the mud by the side of the water. "Yes," said the prisoner, "and there was some there"—indicating a spot on the edge of the pool—"but the police have dug it out."

It looks as if there were some blood on these leaves, too," said the interviewer. It was now too dark to see properly, so young Buckham struck a match, and it was found that the leaves were wet with water, and not with blood. "Have they found any weapon?" Buckham was asked. "No," came the reply, "they have dragged the pond to find one." "It looks like murder to me," suggested the resident. "It does," replied the young man, as he lit a cigarette. It was then remarked that Buckham would doubtless have to be a witness at the inquest. "Perhaps I shall," said he; "what do you have to do there?" It was explained that a witness at an inquest answered to the best of his ability questions that were put to him A policeman then joined the couple, and this particular conversation ended. Buckham was very cool throughout. Little did the man who spoke with him suspect that the young man was likely to be charged with the murder, and he was little less than astounded when he heard in the morning that the police had watched the Buckhams' house all night and had entered at seven a.m. and arrested the brothers shortly afterwards.

Mr. Watson preached at the Christian Mission Chapel on the Sunday evening before he met his tragic end, and in the afternoon he had had some neighbours at his house to tea. The congregation at the little chapel mourned his loss on Sunday last as they assembled for worship, looked upon the spot from which he had so recently addressed them, and thought of what had happened since. Mr. Watson was a nice-looking man, with dark whiskers and short dark beard. His wife was a pleasant-looking woman. Both were hard workers, fond of their little home and the Mission Chapel.

EXTRAORDINARY SCENES ON SUNDAY.

Thousands of people visited the scene of the tragedy on Sunday by all possible means of progression—by train, in motor cars, on motor cycles, in carriages, brakes, wagonettes, on cycles, and even on crutches Rarely have so many bicycles been seen together in a road as were continually wheeled up and down Honeypot-lane. The houses of the murdered couple and the prisoners were stared at from the lane, but the centre of this morbid curiosity was the dark, dank pool where man and wife were shot down. Round this a circle of people were always standing—a circle so far as the trees, brambles, and hedge would allow. In the corner opposite to that from which the gun was pointed men were busy with knives cutting out stakes and parts of bushes, in some of which shot were embedded. From the oak tree overhanging the pool hundreds of branches were pulled as relics of the gruesome tragedy, and such phrases as "I've got a bit of the tree the poor people died under," and "I've got a piece where the bullets drove," were heard on every hand. Cyclists carried away large branches on their machines and from the names on

41 Newspaper coverage of the 'Basildon Murder'. An elderly couple were shot dead by two young boys in Honeypot Lane in August 1906 because they insisted on using water from the boys' father's pond.

42 Cartridges used in the murder of PC George Gutteridge in September 1927. The case broke new ground in ballistic science when markings on the cartridges which killed the officer were matched with others belonging to the killer.

43 The memorial to PC George Gutteridge, murdered at Stapleford Abbotts in September 1927.

In 1926 the General Strike led to another new type of criminal disorder in the county, though this was not as serious as a crime which took place the following year.

The murder of PC George Gutteridge in 1927 is one of the most notorious events in the history of crime in Essex and has become a famous case throughout the police world for the work on ballistics which led to a successful conviction.

Gutteridge was the beat officer at Stapleford Abbotts, where he, his wife and family were well known in the village. In the early hours of 27 September 1927 the officer stopped the occupants of a stolen car at nearby Passingford Bridge and got out his notebook to write down some information. As he did so, he was callously shot twice in the head and he slumped to the ground beside the car. His assailant then knelt over the body and shot the officer twice more—once through each eye. (This latter factor, when it emerged, caused widespread public revulsion and an increased desire to see the criminals caught.) The body was not discovered until 6am, when it was found by the local postal delivery man. A huge murder hunt was immediately initiated.

The car used by the murderers was quickly located. It had been stolen from Billericay and abandoned in South London. Calculations soon revealed that the elapsed time between the theft of the car and the murder of the policeman was approximately as long as it would have taken to drive from Billericay to Passingford Bridge. Bloodstains were found on the driver's side running board and a further, vital, clue was the discovery of a gun cartridge in the car.

Enquiries led to two crooks running a car-stealing-and-selling business—Frederick Browne and William Kennedy. Police visited the premises and arrested Browne on a charge of car stealing. He was searched and some cartridges matching the ones used in PC Gutteridge's murder were found. Kennedy was arrested in Liverpool, where he had tried to shoot another policeman, and he was also charged with stealing a car.

Kennedy subsequently made a full confession, stating that he and Browne had stolen the car from Billericay, intending to take it back to their garage for sale. They had been stopped by an officer at Passingford Bridge and, while the latter was taking notes, Browne suddenly produced a gun and shot him. Browne then got out and fired two more shots into the dying man as he lay on the road.

Browne's gun was found and subsequent examination showed that the cartridges in the gun, those found in his possession and the one found in the stolen car all had the same pattern on them and could all be traced to the same gun. It was sufficient evidence to convict the two men and both were ultimately hanged for the crime.

PC Gutteridge was buried at Warley cemetery after a service at nearby Christ Church. Crowds lined the route as the funeral cortège made its way from a relative's home in Junction Road. Two-thirds of the seats in the church were occupied by uniformed police officers, all there to pay last respects to their colleague.

Crime is not just a historic phenomenon.

In 1972 the family-run Barn restaurant in Rayne Road, Braintree, was raided by two gunmen and three of the family were shot, one fatally. Extensive enquiries eventually tracked down the two gunmen, John Brook and Nicholas de Clare Johnson, who had originally broken into the premises to steal money from the safe. They were convicted in January 1974, when the effects of the case were still being felt around the incredulous neighbourhood.

Ten years later, on 7 August 1985, the crime headlines focused on White House Farm in Tolleshunt D'Arcy, where five members of the

Bamber family were found dead at their family home. It was originally thought that Sheila Caffell, an adoptive daughter with a record of mental problems, had murdered her twin sons and adoptive parents and then killed herself. Several weeks later, however, forensic evidence and detailed investigations led police to Jeremy Bamber, her adopted brother, who was arrested, questioned and ultimately convicted of the crimes.

By an eerie coincidence, one of the most recent Essex cases to hit the national headlines also happened near a White House Farm, this time at Rettendon. In the middle of the night shortly before Christmas 1995, in a dark country lane, three men in a Range Rover, allegedly waiting to complete a drugs deal, were apparently murdered by two members of a rival gang which had set them up.

Such modern-day crimes serve as a painful reminder that, romantic though they might appear now, historic cases like the Victorian 'crimes of passion' murders must have been equally horrific in their day.

44   The lane in Rettendon where three men were killed in 1995 as they waited in a Range Rover, apparently in anticipation of a drugs deal.

CHAPTER III

Earthquakes

Perhaps the most amazing natural event to have affected the county was the great Essex earthquake of 1884.

Earthquakes are more usually associated with areas of high tectonic plate activity, but surprisingly this was not the first event of its kind in Essex—and indeed Britain has had a number of earthquakes dating back to at least A.D. 103.

Before 1884 the most significant Essex earthquake was in September 1692, when St Peter's church in Colchester was very badly hit. The 1884 earthquake also struck the Colchester area, and several villages to the south of the old Roman town suffered extensive damage.

It happened at 9.18am on Tuesday, 22 April 1884. The *Essex Chronicle* of Friday 25 April carried detailed reports from all the affected areas—everywhere there was severe damage and destruction. The church at Langenhoe was completely destroyed and the villages of Wivenhoe, Abberton

45 The parish church at Langenhoe was completely destroyed by the 1884 Essex earthquake and had to be demolished. This picture shows the extent of the damage to the tower, roof and walls.

46 The quay area of Wivenhoe suffered particularly badly, many buildings were damaged and the area was covered in dust and smoke. This picture shows scaffolding on one of the buildings erected to prevent any further movement in the walls.

and Peldon all suffered extensive damage, as buildings throughout the area lost chimneys, roofs and ornamental masonry.

The quay area of Wivenhoe in particular suffered badly, and the houses were lost in a haze of dust and smoke. The recently-restored parish church, the Independent Chapel and the National School

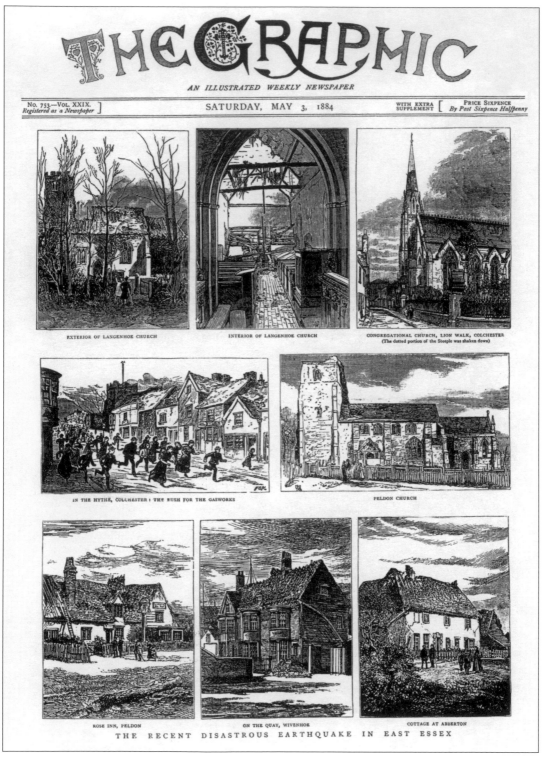

THE RECENT DISASTROUS EARTHQUAKE IN EAST ESSEX

47 The front page of *The Graphic* on Saturday, 3 May 1884, illustrated the extent of the damage throughout the area. 'The rush for the gasworks' at The Hythe, Colchester, was caused by the belief—here as elsewhere—that the cause of devastation had been a gas explosion.

48 The *Bell* inn at Old Heath, Colchester, in the aftermath of the Essex earthquake. Local people heard a tremendous rattling noise and the ground began to shake beneath their feet. Then there was a deathly silence and people began to pour out of their houses into the street. The roof of the *Bell* fell in and most other roofs in the area lost their tiles.

49 The village of Peldon suffered extensive damage from the 1884 Essex earthquake and its church was one of several ecclesiastical buildings in the area to be affected. The end wall of the Church Clerk's House was almost completely destroyed.

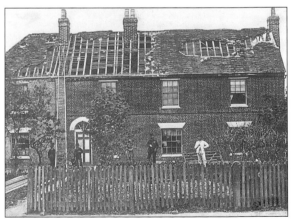

50 Wick Farm, Langenhoe, was one of many buildings which lost their roofs during the earthquake.

were all severely damaged, as were Wivenhoe Hall and the gasworks—many thought that an explosion at the works was the cause of all the damage and destruction. Local doctors were kept busy all day patching up injuries and the following day soldiers

from Colchester barracks came to help clean up the town.

In Colchester itself the spire of the Lion Walk Congregational Church fell to the ground, damaging the nave and smashing some of the gravestones in

51 Several villages south of Colchester suffered earthquake damage. This picture shows Rowhedge, where Mr. Crosby's house—propped up by makeshift scaffolding—was among the worst affected.

the graveyard. The North Station and Hythe areas also suffered and much damage was caused to the *Bell* inn at Old Heath, which lost virtually all its roof. Bells rang out through the town from Colchester's numerous churches as the towers which held them were shaken to the core by underground rumblings.

On Mersea Island huge cracks appeared in the ground and waterspouts issued from them. The churches at Peldon, Layer de la Haye and Little Wigborough all suffered major structural damage; the tower at the latter required substantial rebuilding.

Though the epicentre was in Essex, the earthquake was felt over a 150-mile radius, covering an area of more than 50,000 square miles. Over 1,200 buildings were destroyed and many others were damaged—a considerable number for a shockwave lasting only a few seconds! Modern estimates put it at 5.2 on the Richter Scale (invented in the 1930s).

The devastation caused by the Essex earthquake was estimated at tens of thousands of pounds and a relief fund was set up for the victims with the assistance of the Lord Mayor of London and various Essex MPs. Contributions to the fund were, however, in short supply, as people found it difficult to comprehend that such an event had taken place on English soil. More money would have been raised, lamented Wivenhoe JP, James Jackson, if a fund had been set up for an earthquake in Timbuctoo!

The loss of life in the earthquake was small. There are few reliable reports of any deaths and extensive research has shown that perhaps only two or three people at most were killed. For those who survived, however, there was much to be remembered—the subterranean rumbling (various descriptions compared the sound to an underground steam train, a galloping waggon & horses and the nearby firing of big guns), the shock of the suddenness of it all and the nausea at the wave-like motion which lifted buildings and people and then

THE ILLUSTRATED LONDON NEWS

REGISTERED AT THE GENERAL POST-OFFICE FOR TRANSMISSION ABROAD.

No. 2350.—VOL. LXXXIV.

SATURDAY, MAY 3, 1884.

WITH SUPPLEMENT AND TINTED PICTURE | SIXPENCE. By Post, 6½d.

THE EARTHQUAKE IN ESSEX.

A survey of the area of the greatest severity of the earthquake shock on Tuesday week shows that the extent of the damage is far greater than was supposed from the first vague accounts which came to hand from the district round Colchester. These by no means exaggerated the amount of destruction caused within the small circle in which the influence of the wave was most distinctly felt, but rather erred in estimating the damage too low. From Colchester in a south-easterly direction towards Abberton, the effects of the earthquake are visible on every hand. This little parish is situate about three miles from Colchester, and bears witness in a remarkable degree to the intensity 'of the shock which affected the surface of the country. Not only were chimneys thrown down in all directions, but houses were unroofed, the gable walls cracked, and the foundations shaken. Passing on to Langenhoe, a few miles further on, the most remarkable evidences of the shock are to be seen. Farmhouses are wrecked, or partially so, all along the high road, while Langenhoe Church, an ancient structure of stone built in the Norman period, is shattered in a manner that would scarcely be credited except from personal observation. The massive tower, surmounted by battlements, constructed of great blocks of stone, was so shaken that the heavy masonry fell with destructive force on to the roof above the nave and chancel, utterly destroying the roof for a space of ten feet square, and filling the interior of the edifice with a mass of débris. The Rector, the Rev. Mr. Parkinson, has suffered by the partial demolition of his residence, situate about two hundred yards from the church. There were half a dozen chimney-stacks on the house, and these have all been overthrown or twisted on their foundations so as to necessitate their being removed, while the walls have been cracked in every direction. Long fissures appear also in the grounds surrounding the house, particularly in the hard-rolled gravel walks. Mr. Parkinson says he felt the shock in a series of undulations, accompanied by a twisting motion; the furniture and other articles in the house appearing to perform a gyrating movement, and the whole series of shocks, for there were more than one, lasting about half a minute. Several farmhouses in the vicinity are much damaged by being partially unroofed and by the gables falling out. Altogether the damage in this parish amounts to several thousand pounds. In a southerly direction from Langenhoe lies Peldon, a much larger parish, and the spectacle here from the high road is of an extraordinary character. It is a fact that not a single dwelling or building of any description in Peldon has escaped injury in a greater or less degree. From the church on the hill down to the lowest cottier's dwelling, destruction has been wrought on every hand, the seismic movement exerting itself in some cases in the displacement of masonry and brickwork in the most fantastic forms. The church of Peldon itself, a fine structure built in the thirteenth century, is rendered unfit for present use, the battlements of the Norman tower and the crown having been thrown to the ground or into the body of the building, breaking through the roof in their descent, and smashing the pews beneath. The residence of Mr. Holland, a large house of modern construction, has been shattered from basement to roof almost beyond repair. The walls and staircases have been torn asunder, and the outer walls cracked and split in all directions. It is estimated that the destruction to house property alone in this district will amount to over £6000. As illustrating the peculiarity of the wave in its effects on

LANGENHOE CHURCH, WITH THE RUINED TOWER AND ROOF.

buildings, it may be noted, that a house in Peldon was moved upon its foundation for a space of six inches, not laterally, but as if it had been taken and partially turned round. Some remarkable phenomena were noticed at the village of West Mersea, about six miles from Colchester. The place is supplied with water from a number of natural springs, which produce water of great purity. When the shock took place a great fissure, a rod in length, opened in the ground, and the water in the springs, finding a new channel of escape, was temporarily drawn off from the pools where it had accumulated. The water taken from the wells immediately afterwards was discoloured, some of the samples being of a chalky hue, while others were coloured red, as if they held particles of mineral earth in solution. At the schoolhouse at West Mersea the children, 140 in number, had a narrow escape, the building being partially unroofed, the falling bricks and tiles creating the utmost terror among them; but the master, with great presence of mind, ran to the door as they crowded out and commanded them to return to their seats until they could leave the building in an orderly manner. The residence of Dr. Green at this place is a complete wreck, presenting one of the most startling evidences of the destructive effects of the earthquake. There is not a room that is not damaged, and the building will probably have to come down altogether. Dr. Green had just entered his surgery when the shock occurred, and had a narrow escape from the falling bottles and glasses. It is satisfactory to note that, with the exception of one at Row Hedge, no lives have been lost; which, considering the immensity of the destruction to property, is remarkable indeed. A subscription is opened by the Lord Mayor of London for the relief of the poorer class of sufferers.

SHATTERED HOUSES AT PELDON.

52 The front page of *The Illustrated London News*, one of *The Graphic*'s rivals, giving full details of the earthquake and showing the destruction it caused in two of the most badly affected villages, Langenhoe and Peldon. In an era before photographs were in regular use by newspapers, artists' impressions were the best way of providing people with a graphic representation of significant events.

THE ILLUSTRATED LONDON NEWS, MAY 3, 1881.— 416

EFFECTS   OF   THE   EARTHQUAKE   IN   ESSEX.

COTTAGE, ABBERTON.

AT ABBERTON.

PUBLIC-HOUSE, PELDON ROSE.

PARISH CHURCH, PELDON.

MR. CHARLES HARVEY'S HOUSE, WIGBOROUGH.

COTTAGE, PELDON ROSE.

DOORWAY OF COTTAGE, PELDON ROSE.

MR. NELSON'S, WIG FARM, LANGENHOE.

53   Another page from the same issue of *The Illustrated London News*, showing a range of damaged buildings from Abberton, Langenhoe, Wigborough and Peldon.

promptly reinstated them where they stood. There was much to be repaired amid the constant fear that it would happen again.

The offices of the *Essex Chronicle* were besieged by people eager for news and the Post Office at Colchester handled thousands of telegraph messages to and from the London newspapers.

Over the weekend following the earthquake, hundreds of sightseers arrived in Colchester and Wivenhoe. Among them were several photographers, who captured the scenes of destruction on film—often for conversion into postcards which could be sold to raise funds for rebuilding work—and left a pictorial legacy for us today of this incredible event. Newspapers without photographers sent graphic artists instead to capture every detail.

Apart from the photographs and the drawings, the only memorial to the earthquake is a brass plaque in the tower of Little Wigborough church:

> To the glory of God and in affectionate memory of Juliana Elizabeth Watson the tower of this church was rebuilt out of a bequest left by the late Sophia Watson by the Rev. Frederick Watson M.A., rector of this parish after the earthquake of April 22 1884 in the years 1885 and 1886.

This and other local churches held thanksgiving services and there was much excited talk about earthquakes for many months afterwards.

Nobody who lived through the great Essex earthquake and felt its irresistible power would ever be able to forget it.

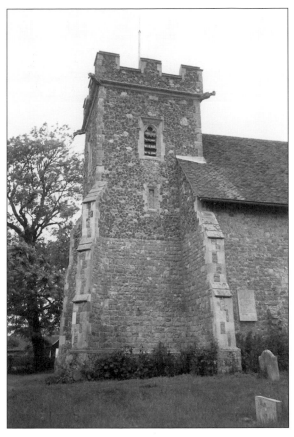

54 A modern photograph of Little Wigborough church, the location of the only known memorial to the 1884 Essex earthquake. Over a century later, the difference between the original stonework of the tower and the stonework of the 1885-6 repair work necessitated by the earthquake can still be seen.

CHAPTER IV

Storm & Flood

For Essex the 1884 earthquake was a rarity. Far more frequent have been the storms and floods bringing havoc to coastal and inland areas alike.

In its position on the east coast of England, Essex is exposed to the rigours of the weather—high spring tides, unseasonal gales or blizzards from Siberia. With the North Sea to the east, and the Rivers Stour to the north, Thames to the south and Lea/Stort to the west of the county, Essex is almost completely surrounded by water. Several major rivers also flow through the county, and much of the land is so low-lying that flooding is highly likely. Nowhere in the county is more than 35 miles from tidal water and, when water levels are high—perhaps after a heavy snowfall or a sudden downpour—and storms whip them into a frenzy, it can only spell disaster. Storm surges funnelling down the North Sea into the county's river estuaries have been a feature of the way of life on coastal Essex for centuries.

Numerous maritime communities, ports, yachting centres and tourist resorts have grown up on the Essex coast and most of them at some stage have been storm-damaged or flooded. Over the years more and more flood defences have been introduced to keep the sea at bay and to protect homes, livelihoods and valuable agricultural land. There is an innate fear of the sea in many Essex coastal communities and one can easily understand why when one looks at the destruction illustrated in these photographs.

The first recorded flooding in the county took place in A.D. 31 but numerous other storms and floods have been recorded by chroniclers in subsequent centuries. The Anglo-Saxon Chronicle and the 13th-century historian Matthew Paris both recorded contemporary disasters. In the 14th century the River Thames suffered several breaches of its walls, whilst in 1570 a 'great storm' brought death and destruction to people, houses and livestock.

The first significant storm in modern times was 'The Channel Storm' of 26 November 1703, which claimed the lives of an estimated 8,000 people throughout the whole of England. Numerous ships around the Essex coast were sunk or damaged, windmills collapsed in their hundreds and many houses were rendered uninhabitable. The Essex inventor, Henry Winstanley, was one of the most famous casualties of this storm, losing his life in the Eddystone lighthouse which was carried away and completely destroyed. Four years later the 'Dagenham Breach' took place, when floodwaters from the Thames spilled disastrously onto adjacent land through a breach in the seawall.

Another major storm took place on 16 February 1736, when strong north-westerly winds and the pull of a full moon combined to create a large tidal surge down the east coast which flooded a huge area from Lincolnshire to Kent. Seawalls were broken down, agricultural land was destroyed and hundreds of people were made homeless. The February issue of the *Gentleman's Magazine* reported that 'the little Isles of Canvey and Foulness were quite under water, not a hoof was saved, and the inhabitants were taken from the upper part of their houses in boats'.

Before the century was out another storm and the continuing process of coastal erosion had claimed Walton church for the sea.

The next major flood came in 1888—'the year without a summer'. Snow fell in Romford, Stock and other places on 11 July and by the end of the month torrential rain and thunderstorms had brought even more misery to Essex's inhabitants. Over four inches of rain fell in five days in Chelmsford and a similar amount in just two days in Ilford. On 1 August rain fell incessantly all day. The rivers and fields could not absorb all the water and by early morning on 2 August the first floodwaters were evident.

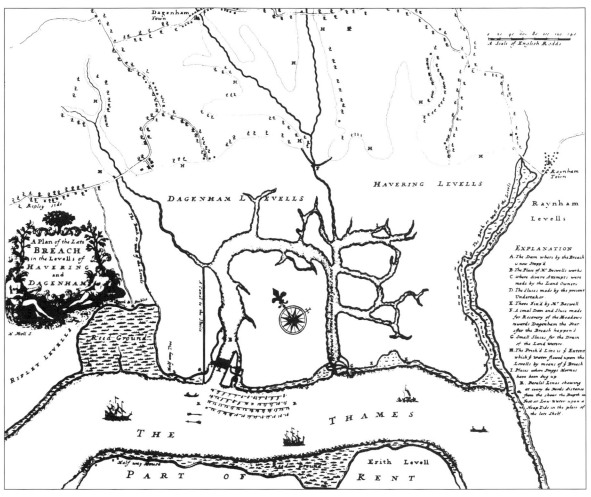

55 A plan showing the effects of the 'Dagenham Breach'—a breach of the seawall on the northern shore of the River Thames in 1707. The key to the plan is particularly enlightening, the dotted line apparently showing 'ye extent which ye water flowed upon the Levells [the surrounding marshland] by means of ye Breach'.

In Chelmsford, the iron bridge in London Road spanning the River Can collapsed as the rushing floodwaters pounded it with uprooted trees and other debris. The older Stone Bridge survived, but was seen to sway and crack as the waters rushed through, and police warned people not to cross it. Streets became swirling rivers and many houses were inundated, some of them to a height of seven or eight feet.

Romford, too, was badly affected. The River Rom burst its banks, carrying off beer barrels from the Ind Coope Brewery and flooding some streets in the town to first-floor level. One sixth of Romford's normal annual rainfall fell in just one day on 1 August and, when the floodwaters had subsided, the brewery—which lost an estimated £30,000 in the disaster—installed a low-level bar across its part of the river to prevent a similar loss of beer barrels.

The *Essex Chronicle* was quick to report on the disaster:

Lamentable weather has again prevailed during almost the whole of this week. Rain has fallen in torrents all over the county and great damage and much inconvenience have been caused by floods. Chelmsford, Romford, Brentwood & neighbourhood, the Barking & Tilbury district and Wethersfield have especially suffered … At Beckton a man was killed by lightning. Others have been injured by the same agency and stacks have been fired. Such hay as remained out has been hopelessly spoiled and some has been washed away down the streams … The earthquake of 1884 … quite pales before it.

56 'The Great Flood' at The Friars in Chelmsford on 2 August 1888, the day after a huge downpour and the culmination of several weeks of torrential rain. The bridge over the River Can in London Road was swept away and a major operation had to be undertaken to rescue people stranded in their houses. 1 August was to go down in history as the wettest day of the 19th century in Essex, but most of the damage was done the following day. The tall building on the left was the National School and the cottages in the distance marked the entrance to the old friary. Everything in the picture has gone and the road has been replaced by the Parkway dual carriageway.

At Stifford a road collapsed, leaving a 25-feet deep hole. In the larger towns sewage was carried through residential streets and there were grave fears about diphtheria and typhoid. The total amount of damage caused by the floods was put at £250,000 and an appeal was made to the Lord Mayor of London for financial assistance. Chelmsford photographer, Fred Spalding, ever one to spot a business opportunity, was soon offering 15 pictures of the floods for sale and some of the proceeds may well have been used to help local flood victims.

In 1897 two freak weather phenomena hit the county. First, on 24 June, two days after Queen Victoria's Diamond Jubilee, a massive hailstorm struck at Ingatestone. Heat and humidity had been building up for days and, when the storm finally hit, it was devastating. Buildings were damaged, trees were felled, crops destroyed, animals killed and fish were blown out of their ponds. An eyewitness, Mr. Coverdale, told how hailstones had riddled his umbrella, making it completely useless, and how his son had been hit on the head, producing a bump as big as an egg. Several hailstones measured six inches round and some were weighed at Ingatestone Post Office at 3.5 ounces each.

At the end of the year another flood—the so-called 'Black Monday' flood of 19 November 1897—wrought havoc throughout the county, particularly in coastal areas. A strong south-westerly gale brought damage and destruction to buildings the previous day, before turning northwards and whipping up sea water to overtop the defences. The *Essex Chronicle* printed a double-page spread about the disaster, under the title 'Terrible Gale And High Tides - Immense Havoc On Land And Sea':

The valleys of the Thames, Crouch, Roach, Stour and Blackwater and the islands lying off the coast, such as Foulness, Canvey and Wallasea, were inundated by high tides, swept by furious winds and turned into scenes of wretchedness and desolation which it is almost impossible to

57 The River Colne at Colneford Bridge, on the boundary between Earls Colne and White Colne. This picture is probably a depiction of the 'Black Monday' floods of 1897, showing how they affected an inland parish. The opportunity to row across the road certainly seems to have attracted some interest! The picture was taken by Charles Skelton Tyler, photographer and pharmacist of Earls Colne throughout the 1890s.

describe … The visitation, there can be no doubt, is a calamitous one and will rank among the most disastrous that has been known in this county within the memory of man.

Much of the Dengie Hundred was under several feet of water, and wild and domestic animals were trapped on isolated land for hours until they could be rescued. Ten soldiers in two boats at Shoeburyness barracks were swept out to sea and carried across to Kent, whilst at Southend many houses were flooded. A newspaper reporter, visiting the town a few days later, recorded that 'high up on the outside of every house on the seafront is an ominous mark, denoting how far the destroying element proceeded, while inside each house there is tumbled wreckage enough to spell a far from happy or comfortable Christmas'. Bathing machines 'floated about like cockleshells', numerous boats were either sunk or damaged and houses in the Lower Town (the seafront area) were flooded with sewage.

Great Wakering, Canvey Island, Bowers Gifford and Burnham-on-Crouch were all badly flooded. The railway line between Pitsea and Benfleet was washed away and at Leigh-on-Sea there were several 'gallant rescues' as people were 'saved from certain death'. The whole of the south and east coast, from Pitsea marshes to Walton-on-the-Naze, was flooded and hundreds of acres of valuable agricultural land were destroyed. Passengers on the Wivenhoe-Brightlingsea railway line had to be transferred from their train into boats. There was even some inland flooding at places such as Colchester, Coggeshall and Earls Colne. The effects of the flood were long-lasting: an estimated 50,000 acres of land were flooded and farming was affected for many years afterwards.

Six years later there were more floods. From 12-20 June 1903 continual downpours caused inevitable flooding. Between Saturday 13 and Monday 15 June there were 59 hours of continuous rain. Areas right across the county, from Saffron Walden in the north west to Southend in the south east, were affected.

58 The 'Black Monday' floods of 29 November 1897 brought severe flooding to many parts of Essex, particularly along the coast. The effects can be seen here on The Quay at Burnham-on-Crouch. This was not the first (or last) time that the quay had been flooded but the 1897 flood was the first Burnham flood to be widely photographed and several pictures of it survive. The building on the left is The Shore House, an 18th-century structure. The floodwaters, seen here overtopping the edge of the quay, would today be repulsed by a modern seawall which runs the length of Burnham seafront.

59 The effects of the 1903 flood at Green Farm, Little Sampford. The River Pant burst its banks and rose several feet in what the sender of this card described as 'one of our weekly floods'. The *Essex Chronicle* reported that there was 'much damage to hay in the Braintree district—some fields are flooded and any cut hay is floating about'. This card was produced especially for Christmas 1903 and New Year 1904, and carries a pre-printed seasonal greeting on the reverse.

The *Essex Chronicle* reported:

the low-lying ground between East Ham and Barking, bounding the old course of the Aldersbrook, behind the old gasworks, was completely submerged, and as of late years it has been covered with houses and other buildings, the distress and damage caused by the flood was very great indeed … Hundreds of houses were flooded over the first floor and the total loss is put at many thousands of pounds.

The south west of the county was hardest hit, and Ilford, Abridge and Buckhurst Hill also suffered.

And so it went on. In 1910 there were storm surges; 1912 flooded streets. In May 1913 storms brought lightning and hail to various parts of Essex, including Wivenhoe and Great Yeldham. On Tuesday 17 June of that year a great storm brought rain, hail and lightning to various parts of north and north-east Essex. In Braintree three men were killed while sheltering in an iron shed after lightning apparently pierced a hole in the roof and struck the

60 Floods, Abridge, 1903

61 The south-west part of the county bore the brunt of the 1903 floods. Romford High Street was impassable and the local fire engine was used to pump floodwater from people's homes. Thousands of pounds' worth of damage was caused at Ilford, including £3,000 worth to the local brickworks, and the new station goods yard was wrecked as soil was washed away. Some residents had to struggle with up to five feet of water. These pictures show the situation in Abridge and Ilford. The children in the Ilford picture are evidently enjoying the novelty of floodwater, but it is unlikely that their parents were quite so cheerful about it!

pitchforks they were holding. In neighbouring Bocking a chimney was split open and a ball of fire, dust and smoke came out in the living room of the house which was hit. Houses and trees were struck by lightning in Witham, a man was struck in Kelvedon, and in Manningtree some chickens were killed by falling hail and lumps of ice. The *Shipwrights Arms* pub in Wivenhoe was badly damaged.

In 1919 it was floods again, as melting snow caused rivers to burst their banks and flood residential streets. The *Essex Chronicle* carried a full-page feature on the flooding, which affected much of the county for several days following a sudden storm comprising lightning, snow and high winds which struck overnight on the weekend of 26-27 April.

Under the headline, 'Wildest Night For Years', the newspaper reported: a girl was carried away and drowned by the floods at Mountnessing and a man died from exposure in Epping Forest. A house in Heybridge was struck by lightning, trees were blown

62 Between the major floods there were several smaller or local inundations. This picture of Westcliff seafront dates from the first decade of the 20th century, and probably from February 1910 when the Southend area was lashed by a fierce storm which whipped the sea up onto the esplanade and damaged some buildings in the town. Despite subsequent improvements to the sea defences, waves still leap onto the esplanade when the tide and wind combine their strength.

63 Unlike Westcliff-on-Sea, Walton-on-the-Naze does not face into the quiet waters of the River Thames but the might of the North Sea. This picture from *c.*1912 shows the danger of a combination of high tide and strong winds. The curious design of the sea defences is supposed to minimise the impact of the thundering waves. This card was posted in August 1912, an unseasonally wet month, and the sender writes, 'it's fine here, but very cold—winter coats out'!

64 Cambridge Road, Clacton-on-Sea, on Monday 26 August. After an overnight downpour residents woke up to flooded houses, and water up to a foot deep seeped through front doors. Possessions were floating around the room. The problem was exacerbated by a blocked storm water outfall pipe and the result can clearly be seen.

67   North Station flood, Colchester, April 1919.

65   The aftermath of a storm in Wivenhoe on 20
June 1913, when the *Shipwrights Arms*—at the junction
of West Street and Bath Street—was struck by lightning.
The tall chimney was part of the shipyard boilerhouse
which stood behind the pub. The road next to the
damaged building had to be closed to protect passers-
by from falling masonry and a policeman was on guard
duty behind the barrier. The *Shipwrights Arms* was
demolished *c.*1955 and the shipyard site is now being
developed for housing.

66   North Station Flood, Colchester, April 1919.

down in Ilford and the lifeboat was called out at
Clacton.

> At North Station, Colchester, there were extreme
> floods, owing to the rapid thaw, and foot
> passengers and cyclists were unable to pass
> underneath the bridge. At noon on Monday the
> water was running down North Station Road in
> such a flood that the tramcars were unable to
> pass beyond Colne Bank Road.

In 1928 there was widespread flooding again,
largely caused by melting snow, this time in
combination with heavy rain. Roads in Braintree and
Dunmow were blocked by melting floodwaters and
the AA and RAC both issued flood warnings. The
River Blackwater was flooded at Maldon and the
Crouch yet again overtopped Burnham's Quay.
Bridgemarsh and Wallasea Islands were flooded, as
were the Hythe area of Colchester and the Wivenhoe
gasworks and railway line. Trees were uprooted and
telegraph poles were down. At Southend the tide was
five feet above average and along the Thames
embankments and in London 14 people drowned. It
was not just the coastal areas that were affected—
flooding became a major problem across Essex. In the
Lea Valley 1,000 homes were inundated. Maldon,
Heybridge and Burnham were all flooded and the
railway line between Colchester and Wivenhoe was
underwater. The floods were so bad upriver in London
that for the first time the government looked seriously
at a unified, countrywide flood defence system.

Nevertheless, flooding still occurred, extensively
in 1947, 1948 and 1949 though it was nothing by
comparison with the disaster that everyone remembers—the 'Great Tide' of 1953.

The Great Tide struck without warning during
the night of 31 January/1 February 1953. A storm
surge down the east coast had been building all day,
as gale force winds whipped up a high spring tide,
and by nightfall tide gauges from Harwich to

68   Driving conditions have always been difficult when the tide is high on the Strood causeway—the only link between Mersea Island and the Essex mainland. The charabanc on the right in this 1923 picture appears to be full of trippers to the island, which had long been a popular local resort. It may well be one of the Mersea, Colchester & District Bus Company's 'Primrose' fleet, which operated from 1918-1935. Like the children in the Ilford flood picture, the passengers appear to be enjoying the occasion, though the man on the front is having some problem with the engine. The seed, corn and coal merchant whose lorry is also caught in the floodwater was presumably not quite as happy as the charabanc passengers.

69   Clacton-on-Sea seafront in the 1920s, probably in January 1928 when a huge storm struck this part of the Essex coast. The *Essex Chronicle* of 13 January recorded huge seas at Clacton after a deep depression had moved into the North Sea a week earlier, causing a southwards storm surge.

70 The 1928 floods at Coggeshall. The River Blackwater burst its banks in the village and made driving conditions extremely hazardous.

Southend were reading well above normal levels. By the time it reached the River Thames the storm surge was eight feet above predicted levels.

The story of the 1953 flood is still fresh in the memory of those who witnessed it. Sea defences were useless and the floodwaters simply washed over them. Harwich, Jaywick, Foulness Island, Wallasea Island, Southend-on-Sea, Canvey Island, Tilbury and Purfleet all suffered extensively. Canvey was particularly critical—it was the middle of the night when the storm surge struck and 10,000 people living on the island were unprepared. The floodwaters were high, fast-flowing and icy cold.

At daybreak, the extent of the disaster was clearly seen. Seawalls on the eastern side of the island, which were lower and less substantial than those fronting the Thames to the south, gave way and water came pouring in, shattering streets, houses and lives. According to one survivor it took six minutes to go from no water to 14 feet of water.

71   Aerial view of 'The Great Tide', Canvey Island, 1953.

72   A flooded street during 'The Great Tide', Canvey Island, 1953.

73   These three photographs (71-3) of Canvey Island during 'The Great Tide' were taken by the South Benfleet photographers, Shiner & Holmes. This was the horrifying scene that many woke to on 1 February 1953. The aerial view shows the extent of the flooding, whilst the two street scenes show the height of the floodwaters and give some feel for the total devastation they brought to everyday life—cars were replaced by boats as the main mode of transport.

74 'The Great Tide' in Northumberland Avenue, Southend-on-Sea, 1953.

75 Southend-on-Sea was also affected by The Great Tide of 1953. The gasworks in the low-lying Northumberland Avenue area were flooded and coke stored there was washed out into the street, to be shovelled up later for home use by grateful local residents! The gasworks' wall also collapsed.

The picture above shows Northumberland Avenue at the junction of Victoria Road; left, the pumping out operations being carried out by the fire brigade, with PC Anderson also in attendance.

The 1953 Great Tide disaster made national headlines and a huge relief operation got underway to rescue those stranded by the floods. The clean-up took months and, once it was over, sea defences around the county were raised and strengthened, just as they had been after previous floods. Over one hundred people died in the flooding, most of them on Canvey, and there was a desperate urgency to ensure that such a tragedy should never happen again.

There have been a few minor floods since 1953, but nothing on the scale of that disaster. However, there was a localised 'flash flood' in Wickford on Friday 5 September 1958 when the town was hit by heavy rain and the River Crouch burst its banks and flooded the High Street. Several people were trapped overnight in the town on the top deck of a double-decker bus as the waters around them rose to a height of six feet. An amphibious vehicle—an ex-Army DUKW—was used to rescue them and to ferry supplies to people throughout the town. Chelmsford was temporarily cut off by road and rail and numerous surrounding villages also suffered flood damage. Several appeals were launched for the victims and the cost of the damage in Chelmsford alone was put at £250,000.

76 'The Hurricane'—
Manchester Drive, Leigh-on-
Sea, 1987.

77 'The Hurricane'—
Library Gardens, Leigh-on-
Sea, 1987.
  Two photographs of the
after-effects of the 1987
'hurricane', as seen by
residents of Leigh-on-Sea on
the morning of 16 October.
The street scene shows
Manchester Drive, where
trees blocked the road for
several hours. The other
photograph shows one of
the much loved cedar trees
in the Library Gardens
which had stood for
centuries until the hurricane
struck.

In more recent times, 1968, 1978 and 1979 have all seen floods and storms. The 1968 floods led to evacuations in Southend, Rochford and Rayleigh, whilst the night of 11-12 January 1978 brought 70-80mph winds and a tide as high as that of 1953 which the improved seawalls repelled.

One modern storm, however, stands out in the memory of all who experienced it—the 'hurricane' of 15-16 October 1987.

As with the floods of 1953, the 1987 hurricane struck overnight. Winds whipped through the streets as people lay sleepless in their beds, listening to tiles falling off their roofs and fearing that their windows would cave in.

The following morning, after a seemingly endless night of raging storms, they awoke to find destruction all around them. Trees were uprooted by their hundreds across residential streets, crushing cars and damaging houses. Chimney stacks fell through roofs. Local rivers were blocked by fallen trees and other debris. Boats were washed up onto the shore or sunk without trace. Telephone lines and overhead railway wires were brought down; ancient woods which had stood for centuries were destroyed in an instant.

The 1953 flood and the 1987 hurricane each brought home to their witnesses a realisation of how powerful the forces of nature really are and how powerless we are to do anything about them. But were their effects any worse than the 'greate storm' of 1570 or the 'Channel Storm' of 1703? We shall never know. Was the 1987 hurricane the last of the great storms or merely the latest in a series? One day, someone somewhere will find out.

CHAPTER V

Ice & Snow

Ice and snow have had an equally devastating—and equally memorable—impact on the county.

Essex was covered by ice and snow during the last Ice Age and several 'glacial erratic' boulders can be found, for example at Ingatestone, Alphamstone, Beauchamp Roding, Magdalen Laver and Broomfield as evidence of this. Nevertheless, ice and snow falls of more modern times have generated most interest, as the camera has been around to capture them for posterity.

Several memorable snowfalls in the 19th century were witnessed. January 1814 was particularly cold and freezing temperatures killed numerous wild animals and birds. Cricketers played an unseasonal game on Gosfield Lake, in a similar winter in 1838,

while in January 1854 there was a heavy snowfall with drifts up to seven feet deep around the county town. The coldest night in Essex's recorded weather history so far was in 1879: minus 21°C on 7 February at Aveley.

One of the earliest notable snowstorms was the 'blizzard of the century' which struck the county on 18 January 1881. It lasted for over 24 hours and buried people, horses, carts, trains and even houses. Many people died from exposure as drifts up to 17 feet deep swept across the county. Many more died at sea, frozen to death or drowned in their vessels. Lifeboat crews sent to help them also perished. Trains were stuck for hours and passengers had to be rescued and taken home on foot.

78 Records show that December 1890 was the coldest December on record in Essex. Pictures of the event—such as this one of the 'Old Railway Station, Manor Park ... photographed during the Great Frost 1890-1'—are rare, but at least some photographic evidence survives. Though the picture shows the snow well enough, it surely gives no feel for the bitterly cold temperatures that accompanied it.

79 Frozen sea, Southend-on-Sea, 1905.

The *Essex Chronicle* of Friday, 21 January 1881 reported that 'the interruption to business has been serious, the damage to property considerable and, most unfortunate of all, there has been a lamentable loss of life'.

Nine years later, in 1890, Essex suffered its coldest December on record as ice blocked local rivers, and fish and birds died in their hundreds. The Rivers Thames, Blackwater and Can all froze in places and from 25 November onwards there were 59 consecutive days of frost, on 27 of which the temperature failed to rise above freezing point during the daytime.

On 16 January 1905 the River Thames froze again and the ice became so thick that people could walk on it. Local postcard publishers were quick to take photographs of the incident.

The winter of 1916–17, too, was long and cold. Frosts continued into April and the low temperatures brought back memories for older residents of the times when 'milk comes frozen home in pail'. One of the latest snowfalls on record struck on 27 April 1919, covering a large area of central Essex with several inches of snow. The floods at Colchester's North Station shown in the previous chapter were largely due to the thaw which followed this unseasonal weather.

One of the most memorable snowfalls took place at Christmas 1927, when gales carried drifts several feet in height across large parts of the county. Roads and railway lines were buried and villages were cut off, as Essex experienced one of its few genuine 'White Christmases' of the 20th century. Bardfield,

80 Frozen sea, Southend-on-Sea, 1905.

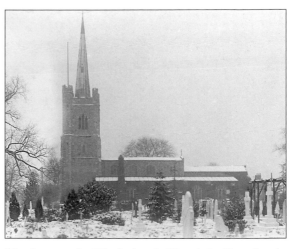

81 The third of three pictures of the frozen sea off Southend-on-Sea on 16 January 1905. The ice was several inches thick and provided local postcard sellers with an ideal subject for publication. Nearby Pier Hill was covered in ice and became extremely hazardous.

82 A postcard of St Andrew's Church in Hornchurch, posted on 13 February 1917. The sender writes, more in hope than reality, that 'the snow has nearly all gone now'.

83 Christmas 1927 was one of the few genuine 'White Christmases' in Essex this century. A heavy snowfall was carried along by strong winds and several villages were cut off by deep drifts. The *Essex Chronicle* reported that 'roads in the Ongar and Blackmore districts were buried to the tops of the hedges and vehicular traffic was seriously interfered with'. This wonderful picture shows the clean-up operation in North Weald Road, Epping, and gives a good indication of just how deep the snowdrifts were.

84 An appropriately seasonal picture of the snow in Epping Forest, the card being posted at Christmas 1927. Smaller settlements like Bardfield and Finchingfield were completely cut off by the Christmas snowfall—a snowfall which had disastrous consequences across the county in January 1928 as the snow began to melt and the rivers to flood.

85 Frozen sea, Leigh-on-Sea, 1929.

86 Frozen sea, Westcliff-on-Sea, 1929.

Two photographs of the frozen River Thames in February 1929—one at Leigh-on-Sea, the other at Westcliff-on-Sea.

Finchingfield and other areas north of Braintree were stranded for several days—supplies ran low and outgoing mail piled high. The south west of the county at Ongar, Epping and surrounding villages was also badly affected.

The *Essex Chronicle* spoke romantically of 'the Great Blizzard' and recorded several 'narrow escapes and remarkable adventures'. Snowdrifts, it noted, obliterated hedges and cars were stuck for hours in the snow. Telephone wires were down and a train on the Bishop's Stortford-Dunmow line was snowed in at the Hockerill halt. Some passengers were sent instead via London and Chelmsford to make sure they got through—a distance of over 100 miles instead of the usual 16 miles! At Little Easton a band hired by the Countess of Warwick for a social event could not get through and in a separate incident a funeral had to be postponed because of the snow.

In 1929 the ice returned to the seaside and, once again, the River Thames was frozen. 12 February was particularly cold, with temperatures dipping to minus 5°C, and waters around the coast froze in their creeks. At Leigh-on-Sea the ice was so thick that it could take a man's weight and many sightseers came out to marvel at the sight. The River Colne also froze and became a temporary skating rink for local people.

One of the best-remembered snowfalls from the post-war years was in January and February 1947. In January gusting east winds brought snow from Siberia that carpeted much of the country and signalled the beginning of seven weeks of turmoil as roads were blocked, powerlines cut and rivers froze. Temperatures dipped to minus 20°C and sporadic blizzards brought two inches of snow to some areas in just 15 minutes. Visibility was reduced to just 20 yards and any thought of travel was useless. At the height of the blizzard snow fell on nine consecutive days and the sun failed to appear for 17 days. Schools were closed, factory workers were laid off and both food and fuel were in short supply.

It was March before the snow abated, but the ensuing thaw caused extensive floods. At least Essex people would soon be comforted by a wonderfully hot summer in what must surely have been one of the most curious years in recorded weather.

Another major snowfall struck during the winter of 1962-3—said to have been the coldest since records began in 1740. Christmas 1962 was certainly the coldest since 1897 and snow fell on Boxing Day at the start of a long sequence of cold weather which would not end until March 1963. In total there were over 60 days when snow was lying on the ground and the sea froze all around the Essex coast. Tem-

87   Dedham High Street on Christmas Day in 1938—another of the 20th century's few 'White Christmases'.

88   The winter of 1962-3 is well remembered for heavy snow and the havoc it caused to daily life. This photograph shows the B183 at Greenhill, Hatfield Broad Oak, on New Year's Day 1963. The machinery being used to clear the road came from nearby Collier Street Farm. Note the sign on the right which is covered by snow.

peratures dropped to minus 20°C and biting 80mph winds made it feel considerably colder. The pattern of 1947 was repeated—roads were blocked, schools and factories were closed, food and fuel were in short supply and snow created drifts several feet high across the county. Large numbers of animals and birds were killed and ice on the Thames at Southend stretched over 600 feet into the estuary.

The winter of 1962-3 is the worst in recent memory, though both those of 1978-9 and early 1987 brought heavy snowfalls and accompanying cold. During the latter period many children enjoyed time off school and, as trains were cancelled and phone lines were down, many adults also enjoyed time off work!

CHAPTER VI

Fire & Explosion

At the opposite end of the spectrum from the cold of ice and snow is the heat of fire, which has been an equal threat to Essex livelihoods. Some of the most dramatic pictures to come out of the county are of fire. This chapter deals with a selection of the major incidents.

By contrast with storms and blizzards, fire is not a wholly natural disaster: it can be caused by direct hits by lightning, human error, electrical faults or deliberate malpractice.

One of the most notable historical fires in Essex was in the first century A.D. when Boudicca (Boadicea) stormed the Roman Colonia at Colchester and set fire to the town.

In the 17th century the south west of the county in particular was probably filled with stories of the 1666 Great Fire of London, as many wealthier Londoners fled for their lives into the surrounding counties during the week-long September conflagration.

Towards the end of the 17th and during the 18th centuries the first step towards modern, professional fire-fighting forces were taken: insurance companies introduced 'firemarks'. These metal plates were fixed to the front of an insured property to indicate to the insurance company's own fire-fighting team that the property was insured with them and that its owners were therefore entitled to assistance in the case of fire. Insurance companies had their own different firemarks and would only protect their own customers' properties. Some of these firemarks can still be seen today on the fronts of older Essex houses.

Fire brigades to protect every property in a parish evolved from the insurance companies' fire-fighting teams, though a countywide fire protection service is a relatively recent innovation.

Two hundred years after the Great Fire of London arson was the most frequent cause of fires: growing unrest among farmworkers and increasingly insufferable burdens on the poor led to riots,

machine-breaking and numerous mysterious fires throughout the county. Many of them were directly attributed to the anger and frustration among the downtrodden masses. Much of rural Essex, where these people lived, suffered severely from arson attacks on farm property and business premises.

In the 1820s the north of the county, where agriculture was more extensive, bore the brunt of this aggression. Towns such as Witham suffered a spate of fires, most of which were attributed to arson attacks by disgruntled farmworkers. Local magistrates and farmers worked hard to resolve the discontent which led people to take the law into their own hands, as organised gangs and unhappy individuals combined to strike terror into the hearts of those with property and money. The local community often turned a blind eye to these illicit, usually night-time, activities and there was uproar in the community when a 16-year-old youth was hanged in 1829 for deliberately firing a barn at Olivers Farm in Witham. Another youth was sentenced to transportation to Australia as the authorities fought to contain the revolt.

There were at least eight apparently deliberate fires in Witham in 1828-29; Finchingfield, Great Yeldham, Rivenhall, Saling and Toppesfield also suffered arson attacks as the unrest continued throughout rural Essex.

In the 1840s there was another spate of fires, this time much more widespread than that of the late 1820s. Communities across Essex—from Great Stambridge to Saffron Walden, from Fingringhoe to South Ockendon—were struck by the firebug and there was great fear amongst landowners and farmers. They were largely caused by farm labourers as barns, haystacks and other farm property were targeted during the night-time. Harsh Poor Laws, great technological advances and an increasing shortage of well-paid work all fuelled growing unrest and the

89   One of many Essex mansions destroyed by fire was Easton Lodge at Little Easton, which fell to the flames in 1847. Its owner, Viscount Maynard, awoke early one Sunday morning to the sound of crackling and, at first thinking it was thieves, went to investigate. He discovered a fire, which he tried to put out with carpets and buckets of water, before being forced to call for assistance from the small lodge fire engine. This was inadequate, so the Thaxted Fire Brigade was called as well. The bell which should have been used to announce a fire was tangled in its ropes, which caused a critical delay. Some paintings and items of furniture were eventually rescued, but the clocktower and much of the main building were destroyed. The *Illustrated London News* observed with regret that 'the flames had made fearful progress, swallowing up in an hour what centuries had spared'.

situation reached a peak in 1844 when 58 apparently deliberate fires were reported in the county. West Bergholt, Braintree, Halstead and Manuden were particularly badly hit during this decade.

In more recent times accidental fires have grabbed the headlines. Several of Essex's ancient mansions, such as Easton Lodge at Little Easton and the Copped Hall in Epping have fallen foul of the flames. A hairclip used as a fuse wire is said to have been the cause of the fire which destroyed the Copped Hall on Sunday 5 May 1917. The popping of bottle corks in the cellar below the smouldering ruins could be heard for days afterwards.

One of the most frightening types of fire in the early days of firefighting was the 'village fire', when a whole village could be threatened by a potential conflagration. Thatch and wood were traditional building materials in Essex, and so the risk of a multiple fire in a close-packed community was very high. One such incident happened on Monday, 18 March 1907 at Debden, where a chimney spark fired a cottage in the main street and a roaring gale carried the flames to neighbouring properties. 'Havoc and panic' set in amongst the residents as the fire extended to buildings on both sides of the road and rapidly destroyed 12 houses. The Saffron Walden and Bishop's Stortford Fire Brigades were called and managed to contain the fire, but even so over fifty people were made homeless and had to be found temporary shelter in neighbours' houses or at the local school. One householder suffered a double tragedy when his carefully-rescued possessions, moved to the safety of a nearby field, were themselves fired by a spark from the burning buildings.

Equally fearful is the fire that destroys a school; this happened at the Church of England School in Wickford on Friday, 10 January 1908.

Fortunately, there was no loss of life. The children were evacuated and sent home as soon as the fire was spotted. This was just as well, for the incident developed into a farce: the fire brigade from Chelmsford refused to turn out because the telegram summoning them did not carry a signature and it was therefore not certain who would

90 Serious damage to the *Salisbury Hotel* in Butt Road, Colchester, shortly after the turn of the century. A gas explosion caused the first-floor wall to blow out.

91 The scene of the 'village fire' at Debden in March 1907. The speed of destruction was exacerbated by a following gale which drove the fire through the village, rich in thatched properties, whose roofs proved easily combustible. Lord Strathcona, who owned many of the damaged buildings, set his bailiff to work to provide shelter for the unfortunate villagers at Debden Hall and on farms on his estate. Damage was estimated at £1,200, then a large expense.

92 The Wickford School fire of January 1908. Children had to be taught in temporary village accommodation while the school was being rebuilt. The site is now occupied by the Church of England Infants School.

pay their expenses. The brigade from Billericay was called instead but, despite arriving 'with commendable promptness' (inside an hour), the school had been virtually destroyed by the time they reached it.

The fire is thought to have been caused by a spark from the chimney which set alight the thatched roof of the building. A new extension to the school had only recently been completed.

Another Friday fire in 1908 broke out at Dedham Mill. On the evening of 19 June, it was reported by the *Essex Chronicle* under the headline 'Disastrous Fire In Constable Country'. A huge crowd was attracted to the scene by the glare from the inferno, the 'colour effects' of which, according to the newspaper, were 'wonderful' to behold!

Manningtree Fire Brigade, led by Captain Seager, used the adjacent River Stour as a water supply to quench the flames; some books and papers were rescued and horses were freed from their stables. Nevertheless the wheat store (where the fire started), the engine house and the engines were completely destroyed. The cost of the damage was put at £40,000. The cause of the fire is thought to have been electrical, as the mill had recently been fitted with electric lighting.

One of the best remembered early 20th-century Essex fires was at Wilson's Corner in Brentwood on Saturday, 9 September 1909. The Great Eastern Stores, owned by Messrs. W.A. Wilson & Co., stood at a prominent road junction in the town (still known as 'Wilson's Corner') and contained seven departments ranging from hardware to furniture to ironmongery. The building was several storeys high, and

93 Dedham Mill was destroyed by fire in June 1908. It was owned at the time by Ebeneezer Clover, whose family occupied both it and its rebuilt replacement for several generations.

94   Wilson's Corner fire, Brentwood, 1909.

had a prominent clocktower facing down Brentwood High Street.

The store's owner, Mr. Wilson, who lived in an adjoining property, was alerted at about 6am, when smoke was seen billowing from one of the cellars. He, with some of the assistants who lived on the premises, tried to contain the fire before the Brentwood Fire Brigade arrived. Unfortunately, however, the cellar was used for the storage of paint and other oil products and these highly flammable materials soon took hold.

As the fire grew, more and more fire brigades were called, and those from Romford, Billericay, Little Burstead, the County Asylum and Warley Barracks were all present. Hundreds of onlookers began to arrive and the whole town came to a standstill as the firemen helplessly fought the growing blaze.

It took until lunchtime to get the fire under control, but by then most of the building had been destroyed. The afternoon was spent pulling down the masonry and by evening only three external walls and a few pillars were left standing. The ruins of the building were still smoking the following day.

The fire is thought to have been caused by a spark in one of the oil or paint cans. The extent of the fire at the time was blamed on the inadequacy of the water supply from the water company. Damage was estimated at £20,000 at least.

Another fire broke out in 1909 at Courtauld's Silk Mills in Chapel Hill, Braintree, on the evening of 9 December. At around 8.40pm the manager,

95   Wilson's Corner fire, Brentwood, 1909.
Two photographs of the 1909 fire at the Great Eastern Stores in Brentwood, owned at the time by Messrs. W.A. Wilson & Co. The road junction still bears the name 'Wilson's Corner'.

96 An artist's impression of the 1909 fire at Courtauld's Silk Mills in Braintree. The new mill was completely destroyed, but the old one was saved by the brave and timely intervention of local firemen.

Mr. Holroyd, had his attention drawn to it by the whimpering of the nightwatchman's dog, a border collie called 'Prince'. Mr. Holroyd sounded the factory hooter, the signal for a fire alarm, and by 9pm Braintree Fire Brigade had arrived to fight the blaze alongside the factory's own fire-fighting unit.

The fire broke out on the second floor of the 'new' mill, built in 1903, and quickly spread along its 900-feet length. It started in the silk spinning room, apparently due to the spontaneous combustion of silk waste. The head of the firm, Samuel Augustine Courtauld JP, arrived at the scene in evening dress, having been called away from a prize-giving ceremony for Braintree Territorials at the Institute Hall.

The fire brigade's tactic, under the direction of Captain Fred Rudkin, was to isolate the fire in the new mill and prevent it from spreading to the adjoining old mill, which dated from 1810 and was one of the oldest such mills in the country. Fireman Harry Willis bravely fought the fire from the walkway between the two mills whilst his colleagues doused him with water to protect him from the fire.

The whole event lasted several hours and attracted numerous local people, including some who had been at the Institute prize-giving and several police officers from surrounding villages. At one stage the flames rose so high they could be seen from Chelmsford, over 10 miles away. Bocking Fire Brigade also arrived, and were soon working with their fire-fighting colleagues to take water from the nearby River Brain and pour it onto the flames.

By morning the fire-fighters had saved the old mill but the new one had been completely destroyed. The combustible silk and crepe had easily burned, whilst the metal machinery used in the manufacturing process had been twisted into garish shapes. Many

of the 500 employees arrived at the gates to find their factory and livelihoods in ruins—and with Christmas approaching there was serious concern and compassion for their plight.

Samuel Courtauld was very sympathetic towards his workers and quickly put in action plans to restore the business. By Monday 200 of the factory girls could be accommodated in the old building, whilst others found jobs at the firm's Halstead mill or worked a shift system at the old mill. Local people started a relief fund to help those most in need. It was reckoned that it would take a year to rebuild the factory, but with spirit and determination the business was able to continue in the meantime.

The factory survived this disaster and Courtauld's business continued to prosper for several more decades.

The following year, another memorable fire took place in nearby Witham. In the early hours of the morning of 9 February 1910, fire was seen coming out of the roof of the Constitutional Club in Newland Street. The club was widely regarded as

97 A photograph of firemen tackling the Constitutional Club fire at Witham in 1910. The building was completely destroyed and never rebuilt.

98 'Village Fire', Little Chesterford, 1914.

99 'Village Fire', Little Chesterford, 1914.

100 'Village Fire', Little Chesterford, 1914.
  Three photographs of the Little Chesterford 'Village Fire' of April 1914. The extent of the damage can clearly be seen. The fire was one of the most widely photographed of its type in the early years of the century and several pictures of it survive.

'the best political club premises in Maldon division' and a lot of money had recently been spent on improvements. It was a landmark in the town—its clock was one of the best-known features of the main shopping street.

The boy who noticed the fire alerted a passer-by and between them they called the local police and the Witham fire engine. The fire brigade from Maldon was also summoned. In the end, however, there was little they could do and the building was totally destroyed. It was never rebuilt and its site is now an open space in front of the United Reform Church (formerly the Congregational Church).

The most likely cause of the Witham fire was a slow-combustion stove which was never allowed to go out as it kept the interior of the building constantly warm. The caretaker, Miss West, lost most of her belongings in the fire.

The Constitutional Club was undoubtedly a big loss to the town, but not as big as the loss which a village in north Essex suffered a few years later. The 1907 'village fire' at Debden created extensive panic at the time. At 11am on Tuesday 7 April 1914 there was equal panic at nearby Little Chesterford when the whole of the main village street went up in flames. Forty people—including a 101-year-old lady—were made homeless as fire swept the length of the village.

The fire at Little Chesterford was probably caused by a spark from a steam lorry passing along the main road next to Bordeaux Farm at the west end of the village. A westerly gale soon carried the flames to neighbouring Manor Farm and onward up the village street. Flames leaped from building to building. Twenty stacks and numerous farm outbuildings were destroyed, as well as eight cottages and two public houses—the *Crown* inn and the *Bushel & Strike* beerhouse. Some substantially constructed buildings survived, including the parish church (which had been in the path of the fire). One or two of the villagers' cottages were also miraculously spared as the flames leapt over them onto neighbouring properties. Many items of furniture were saved and were piled high on the greensward in the street.

The fire was fought by the Saffron Walden, Sawston, Great Chesterford and Audley End brigades and the River Cam nearby was used as one of the principal water sources. At least nine police officers were present, but there was little they could do.

'The village presents a deplorable sight,' lamented an *Essex Chronicle* reporter later, 'but it is a remarkable thing that some of the thatched houses in the path of the fire escaped.'

101 The fire at Pear Tree House, Great Waltham in 1924, when fire-fighters failed to save the roof of the building.

By a strange coincidence, two other fires broke out that week in nearby villages—at Ashdon and Newport. *The Three Tuns* inn at Newport and two neighbouring cottages were completely destroyed, the cause apparently being a spark from a passing train.

As fire prevention techniques and fire-retardant building materials improved, the incidence of village fires became less likely. However, thousands of fires in Essex over the centuries have affected properties large and small, and many more recent fires have been caught on camera. Homes, shops and industry have all been affected, not least during the Second World War, when aerial bombing was the principal cause.

Dedham, site of the 1908 mill fire, suffered again in 1976 when part of the High Street went up in flames. 'Rays of Dedham'—an ancient cloth industry building—was one of the shops destroyed in the fire which cast a shadow over the popular tourist village for some time afterwards.

102 The aftermath of a fire in Dedham High Street in 1976. 'Rays of Dedham', an ironmonger's shop housed in an old cloth industry building, was one of the principal victims.

103 An aerial view of the fire at Southend Pier on 29 July 1976. The pierhead is completely ablaze, despite the work of the fire tug at the bottom of the picture. The fire is thought to have been started either by a lighted cigarette or an electrical fault.

104 The aftermath of the pierhead fire at Southend in 1976. Smoke still hangs around the ruins.

105   The ruins of the bowling alley at the landward end of Southend Pier, which was destroyed by fire in summer 1995. As with many such disasters, a crowd soon gathered to witness the event.

Perhaps one of the most memorable, headline-making fires of modern times was the Southend Pier disaster of 29 July 1976, when a raging summer fire completely consumed the pierhead buildings. It is thought to have started in a bar and to have been caused either by an electrical fault or by a lighted cigarette. Pier trains were quickly used to evacuate tourists and to carry firemen to the scene and waterborne fire-tugs were also called into action. Overhead, a light aircraft dropped water onto the blaze. Smoke from the pier could be seen for miles around and hundreds of people lined the seafront to witness what seemed to mark the end of an era in

the pier's long history. Another fire at its landward end in summer 1995 completely destroyed the bowling alley, but as a result people could look anew at the building and propose new attractions for both ends of the structure.

The destruction of Southend Pier is perhaps the greatest symbol in modern times of the power and unpredictability of fire. Though the pierhead has since been re-decked and there are plans for its future, it has never been completely rebuilt. Perhaps more than anything else, it stands as a stark reminder of the fear and destruction caused by fire.

CHAPTER VII

Road Accidents

The previous chapter described the regrettably long history of fire damage in the county. By comparison, road accidents are a recent phenomenon. Such accidents are now amongst the most common in Essex: motorway accidents, including those on the Essex stretches of the M11 and M25, are regularly featured on television and in the newspapers.

Accidents on the road are mostly within living memory, involving cars, lorries and even trams.

Here is a small selection of the most interesting Essex accidents to have been captured on camera.

On the blustery night of 27 December 1913, Barking tram No.7 was caught in a gale and overturned as it passed along Jenkins Lane in East Ham. It fell into a ditch alongside the track and landed on its side. Fortunately there were no passengers on board at the time and the only damage was a few broken windows. It was soon pulled upright again and put back in service.

106 Barking tram No. 7 lies forlornly on its side in a ditch in Jenkins Lane, East Ham, where it was blown over by a gale on 27 December 1913.

107 A bus crash in Station Road, Westcliff-on-Sea, on 4 December 1914. Note the window sticker advertising the fare—'1d all the way'!

108 A lorry accident at Gun Hill, Dedham, *c.*1921. This picture was taken for John Bowren Lawrence, who ran a grocery and drapery business in nearby Stratford St Mary from *c.*1888 to *c.*1922.

109 An unusual photograph of an accident involving a bus and a wedding car, taken in Pall Mall, Leigh-on-Sea in 1936.

110 The end of the road for a stolen police car, taken from the central police station yard at Southend-on-Sea and driven through a wall in Alexandra Road, *c*.1947. Police are starting to remove the vehicle, whose joy-riding driver evidently missed a massive sign which said 'Dead End' on the other side of the wall in the left of the picture.

Twelve months later, on 4 December 1914, a Tilling Stevens-bodied bus ran off the road at Station Road in Westcliff-on-Sea and met a similar fate, landing in a ditch near Westcliff station. It seems to have been one of the most widely photographed early traffic accidents and several pictures of it survive.

In the early 1920s one of the most dangerous spots in the county was the notoriously steep and winding Gun Hill at Dedham, where several accidents took place. The tollhouse on the River Stour at the bottom of the hill was frequently damaged by wayward vehicles. The road was later straightened and part of the hill was cut away to reduce the gradient, but this only met with limited success. In 1921, for example, a 4½-ton AEC lorry overturned on a bend and ended up on its side next to the tollhouse.

Other unusual road accidents in the county include the time in 1936 when an AEC Regal bus collided with a wedding car in Pall Mall, Leigh-on-Sea, and both vehicles ended up on the pavement. The cause of this accident is unknown, but it was again widely photographed by local people.

In 1947 a police car was stolen by a civilian from the police station yard in Southend and driven, presumably deliberately, into a wall at the end of Alexandra Road in the town. The wall was demolished and the car required substantial repair.

In March 1953 another unusual accident took place in the Southend area—a bus ran into a crane in thick fog on Southchurch Boulevard. Eight people were injured and the top deck of the bus was completely destroyed.

111 An unusual collision in Southchurch Boulevard, Southend-on-Sea, on 2 March 1953, when the jib of a crane pierced the top deck of a bus passing along the Boulevard in thick fog.

CHAPTER VIII

Railway Disasters

More dramatic than road accidents have been the numerous railway disasters on Essex lines since the first track in the county, the London-Romford section, was constructed in 1839. This became part of the main south-west to north-east line, which was extended over the next few years to Brentwood (1840), Chelmsford (1842) and Colchester (1843). The other main line in the county was along the western border, from London to Cambridge, which reached Bishop's Stortford (just over the Hertfordshire border) in 1842 and Audley End, near Saffron Walden, in 1845. Many others, including the notable London-Tilbury-Southend line, were constructed before the 19th century was out, though many smaller branch lines were closed by the Beeching Axe in the 1960s.

The earliest notable Essex rail crash was probably the Kelvedon disaster of 17 October 1872. The 9.45am Yarmouth-London fast train came off the rails immediately north of Kelvedon station when, according to a passenger's account, the track seemed to drop suddenly and the train split in half; one of the carriages toppled over and rolled down the embankment. One person died in the accident and another 16 were injured.

Captain W.H. Tyler held an inquiry into the disaster and the precise cause of the crash was ultimately put down to 'weakness and failure of the leading traverse springs of the engine', which had presumably resulted in the sudden drop felt by the passenger.

In August 1888 the floods which brought havoc to large parts of Essex also affected the county's rail network. A train left the line between Thorpe-le-Soken and Clacton-on-Sea when floodwater loosened the track and undermined its foundations. Eleven people were injured.

The first significant 20th-century train crash in Essex was the widely-photographed 1905 Cromer

Express disaster at Witham. The train left the rails while passing through Witham station on its way to Cromer at around 10.30am on Friday 1 September. Its 14 carriages broke apart and several of the central carriages overturned or landed on the platform. At least 10 people were killed, including the station's foreman porter, Josiah Doole, and perhaps up to 60 were injured. The engine had not been due to stop at Witham and was travelling at between 50 and 70mph when it left the track. A train from the opposite direction—due to pass the Express in Witham station—was fortunately running a couple of minutes late, otherwise the death toll could have been considerably higher.

Local doctors were quickly on the scene and the injured were taken to the Corn Exchange for treatment before transfer to hospital. An eyewitness described it as 'like scenes in the Russo-Japanese War'. The passengers included holidaymakers, notably a party of Felixstowe-bound Barnardo's children in the rear of the train who were fortunate to escape serious injury. The Queen sent a message of sympathy.

A long inquiry, later reopened, eventually concluded that some platelayers, who had been working on the track minutes before the Express appeared, had not properly tightened one of the keys which held it in place.

The 1905 Cromer Express disaster was not the only one of its kind on that route. On 2 March 1907 a London-bound Saturday morning service collided with a truck at Chelmsford 'which was left by some unfortunate overnight on the up-line'. The incident took place near the viaduct which carries the line over the River Can, on the London side of Chelmsford station, but the scale of the disaster was fortunately minimised by the quick reactions of the engine driver who saw the truck on the line ahead as he came out of a bend. The truck was dislodged from the rails, but

112 & 113   Cromer Express disaster, Witham, 1905.

Two pictures of the wreck of the Cromer Express at Witham station on 1 September 1905. The central section of the train left the rails, causing extensive damage and loss of life. The sixth carriage (shown here) mounted the platform and overturned, 'smashing into matchwood under the weight of the undercarriage, bogeys and wheels'.

114 The Chelmsford rail crash of 2 March 1907 was one of several on the London-Colchester mainline. This picture was taken in the early afternoon, some three or four hours after the collision, when a breakdown gang and steam crane were removing the damaged truck. The engine was later taken to Stratford for repair.

the 12-carriage passenger train was only slightly damaged. Nevertheless, those on board were so relieved that many of them got out to shake hands with the driver, who is said to have knelt and prayed by the trackside in thanks for his safe deliverance.

The carriages were taken back to Chelmsford by another engine and passengers were able to continue their journey on the new train which was re-routed to the Capital via the down-line. The driver was given 10 guineas in recognition of his prompt action and alertness.

Six years later an even worse disaster befell the Cromer Express when on Saturday afternoon, 12 July 1913 a London-bound express collided with a local train at Colchester's North Station. The death and destruction were on a similar scale to the Witham disaster, with three killed and 20 injured.

This crash was also the subject of an inquiry, but this time the findings very clearly revealed the cause. The local signalman, who had a long and very good record of work on the railway, seems to have had a momentary lapse of memory and left the local train, which was doing some shunting and had gone to take in water, on the main track which was due to be occupied by the Cromer Express. The driver of the local train saw the signals change, realised the danger and tried unsuccessfully to alert the signalman to his position. Stuck where he was, he decided to try to outrun the Express, to get out of its way, but the latter was upon him before he could move more than 25 yards.

The Express engine—a new one that had only been in service six weeks—was completely destroyed and three of its crew were killed (though an apprentice inspector, making his first journey on the footplate, 'miraculously survived'). The back end of the train remained intact and rescuers found some ladies sitting happily doing crochet work in

115 Cromer Express disaster, Colchester, 1913.

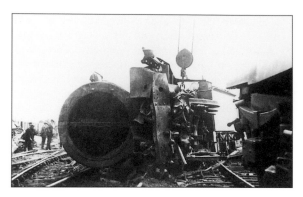

116 This picture and picture 115 show the result of the Colchester railway disaster of 12 July 1913, when the Cromer Express collided with a local train which the signalman had left on the main line. The front coaches of the Express were smashed to pieces. The engine toppled onto its side and had to be removed by a crane.

day. The tailback on the mainline alone—excluding the branch lines—was estimated at 15 miles and some trains took nine hours to travel just 50 miles. At night, the light from the stranded trains lit up the countryside and restaurant cars, station buffets and even local farms were raided for food as hungry passengers sought nourishment. Many walked home instead and still arrived before their train!

The Colchester signalman who had caused the accident was allocated to other duties, but the driver of the local train was commended for trying to avert the disaster. It is generally thought that the number of lives lost would have been even higher if he had not tried to take some evasive action. Reference was made to the disaster during Sunday morning services at Colchester's St Mary-at-the-Walls and Lexden churches.

the rear carriage, completely unaware of what had happened at the front of the train!

The accident led to huge delays on the county's main line and thousands of people were forced to spend the night on stranded trains. The Continental Boat Train, which had a connection to make, was somehow re-routed through the Colchester goods yard, but most had to stay put until the following

Two years after the Colchester train crash there was a disaster at Ilford. The accident took place on 1 January 1915 when, as at Colchester, an express train collided with a local engine. The local train was crossing the main line at about 8.40am when the express from Clacton ploughed into it. According to the *Essex Chronicle* 'the express split the local train in two, literally smashing one carriage to atoms and overturning another, then plunged off the line and toppled into a coalyard below the embankment'.

117 New Year 1915 started badly at Ilford where two trains collided on 1 January in poor visibility as a local train was crossing the main line ahead of a faster express. This picture shows both trains locked together in a hideous tangle, whilst damaged rolling stock and rescuers can also be seen in front of the carriages in the distance on the left.

Several people who saw the crash from Ilford station ran to assist, but there was little they could do. 'Wreckage was piled up in masses and the cries of the injured lying beneath the debris were pitiful in the extreme.' The local newspaper, the *Ilford Recorder*, was even more melodramatic than the *Chronicle*, reporting that 'screams for help proceeded from the living, some of whom were imprisoned with the voiceless dead'. Shutters from Ilford station bookstall were used as stretchers and the police, fire brigade and local Territorials all took part in the rescue. Ten people died, and at least 80 were injured.

The collision was largely caused because the express driver missed a signal, as conditions of poor visibility were made worse by smoke hanging around the express's boiler. The accident was described as 'one of the most serious ever experienced in Britain'.

The London-Colchester mainline was not alone as a victim of disaster. Dagenham Dock on the London, Tilbury & Southend line was the site of the next major train crash in the county, when dense fog on 18 December 1931 was largely responsible for another collision. The back carriages of a goods train heading towards West Thurrock became separated from the rest of the train due to a defective coupling and unbeknown to the driver were then lost in the fog. The guard in the van at the very back of the train was expecting to stop at a signal in the vicinity in any case, so appears to have been unaware that anything was wrong. He only found out when he was hit from behind by another train. Two people died in the collision, including the guard.

Ten years later, on Monday, 10 February 1941, Harold Wood was in the spotlight, because of a collision in which a Southend-bound train ran into another one bound for Norwich. The Norwich train was heavy and the poor wartime coal that was its source of power proved insufficient to get it up the hill between Harold Wood and Brentwood. Eventually it came to a complete standstill and the following train ran into its back. The rear carriage was completely destroyed and at least six people were killed.

Members of the Armed Forces travelling on the trains helped with the rescue, whilst people living nearby contributed refreshments and equipment.

Injured passengers were taken to Warley Wood and Brentwood District Hospitals.

Incidents continued after the war. On Thursday, 2 January 1947 fog at Gidea Park was again primarily responsible for a collision, when a Peterborough express ran into the back of a semi-fast train to Southend. The Peterborough train was late leaving Liverpool Street and the Southend train had been given precedence on the main line until it reached Gidea Park. Held up by fog, it was further hampered by inadequate fog signalling arrangements at Romford, where warning equipment was apparently not put in place in time before the Peterborough express came through. At Gidea Park they collided, the Peterborough train crashing into the back of the Southend one, by then waiting to cross onto the local line. One carriage of the Southend train was thrown through the roof of the station canopy and debris from both trains was piled on the platforms for hours afterwards. The *Romford Times* described the incident as 'the most tragic rail disaster ever in this area'.

Three years later the Peterborough-London mail train ran into the back of a goods train about half a mile from Witham station. A guard and fireman were killed and six coaches were wrecked. Coincidentally an engine derailment had taken place at the station the previous day and one local railway worker, fearing that accidents at the station were becoming a bit too frequent, had ironically joked with his colleagues that he would 'see you tomorrow' for yet more track repairs, not realising then that his services would indeed be required before the day was out.

Finally, yet another collision in fog. In January 1958 outside Dagenham East station a train heading from Fenchurch Street to Shoeburyness ran into the back of a stationary train bound for Thorpe Bay. The rear coaches of the front train were crushed and 10 people lost their lives. A further 90 were injured and the line was not reopened until the following afternoon.

Despite these disasters, train travel remains one of the safest modes of transport available in the county. Thousands of people are moved around Essex every day without incident, and commuting to work by train and touring the more rural areas by rail are both likely to remain popular for many years to come.

CHAPTER IX

Shipwrecks

Essex's position as a coastal county has often left it open to the ravages of the sea. Floodwaters encroaching on land have claimed Essex lives: but those who sail around the county's coasts have also been victims of the water and there have been several memorable shipwrecks.

Not often can one speak of a shipping accident in the same breath as the *Titanic*, but the paddlesteamer *Princess Alice* was the *Titanic* of its day.

The ship, in the early evening of 3 September 1878, was returning from a daytrip from London to Sheerness via Gravesend, where an unexpectedly large number of passengers climbed aboard. At around 6.30pm the steamer entered the stretch near Barking

Creek, navigating by lights as it was now getting too dark to see clearly ahead.

All of a sudden, a collier, the *Bywell Castle*, loomed up out of the darkness from the Millwall Dock and crashed into the pleasureboat's starboard side, splitting it apart in an instant. There was no time to release the lifeboats and within a matter of minutes the *Princess Alice* had sunk without trace.

There were 900 people on board the steamer and most of them disappeared into the water. Other boats in the locality came quickly to their aid, but within 10 minutes an eerie silence had descended over the scene and the rescuers began to fear the worst. Over 600 people were drowned in the disaster.

The Thameside towns of Rainham, East Ham and Barking were deeply affected by the tragedy and a subscription fund was started in honour of the bereaved.

118 The wreck of the *Duchess of Kent* in the River Thames off Grays. As a maritime county, Essex has always suffered heavily when ships have been lost.

119 *Princess Alice*—forward section, River Thames, 1878.

This was the worst-ever shipping disaster (in terms of loss of life) when it happened and it was still third in the all-time list after the *Titanic* went down in 1912. It made headline news and led to the introduction of some new navigation byelaws in the Thames.

One of the most enduring reminders of the power of the sea compared with the inconsequence of man can be found in the parish church of All Saints at Brightlingsea, where a series of wall tiles records every sinking that has affected Brightlingsea townsfolk since 1872. The idea was instituted by the then vicar, Arthur Pertwee, and the tiles commemorate (amongst others) a victim of the *Titanic* disaster itself and numerous seamen from several different ships who all lost their lives in a big storm on 6 March 1883.

The sandbanks off the eastern Essex coast of the county have been a major cause of local shipwrecks. In December 1891 the *Enterkin* was wrecked in a gale off the Galloper Sands, and 30 lives were lost. In January 1899 several other ships were lost in a gale on the nearby Sunk Sand sandbank.

As ships became larger and stronger, there was still no guarantee that they would be safe from the sea. On Friday, 5 May 1905 the armoured cruiser HMS *King Alfred* provided some unexpected interest for Southend residents when it ran aground on sandbanks off the coast of Shoeburyness.

The ship, which was on its way from Chatham to relief duty in the Mediterranean, was caught by a change of current in otherwise calm conditions. Crowds soon gathered on the beach at Shoebury and along Southend Pier to witness the efforts to refloat the ship using tugs from Sheerness (in Kent).

120 *Princess Alice*—aft section. Two pictures of the *Princess Alice* disaster on the River Thames in 1878.

The engraving is taken from the *Illustrated London News* and shows the forward section of the ship and the attempt to rescue people from it on the evening of the accident. The (extremely rare) photograph shows the aft section, beached in the Thames after the collision.

Plans to put the engines full astern and tow it off the sand proved fruitless and it was 1am on Saturday morning before the ship could be refloated. The soft sandbanks caused no damage to the hull and the vessel was able to continue its journey on the Sunday.

Three years later, on 23 November 1908, a Thames Conservancy ship, the *Marlborough*, was torn from her moorings by a gale and thrown through the pier at Southend-on-Sea, causing a gaping hole in the pier decking and substantial structural damage. Some of the supporting piles of the pier were swept away, along with the wooden decking and railings. The cost of repairs was estimated at £600-£700.

121 Part of the frieze of 'shipwreck tiles' around the walls at All Saints' Church, Brightlingsea. The tiles commemorate Brightlingsea men lost to the sea since 1872. A particularly disastrous day was 6 March 1883.

122 The grounding of the HMS *King Alfred* in May 1905 created much interest among Shoeburyness townsfolk. Fortunately it suffered only minor damage and was soon refloated.

123 A classic photograph of the damage caused to Southend Pier by the untethered ship *Marlborough* in November 1908.

124 Another Southend Pier collision—this time featuring the *Violette* in 1921.

After crashing through the pier the *Marlborough* was carried eastwards for several miles until it was brought under anchor again at Shoeburyness. A Leigh bawley also damaged the pier during the same storm and several local yachts were swamped or overturned.

This was not the first time that a ship had collided with the mile-and-a-quarter long pier—it happened in 1895, 1898 and 1907—and it would not be the last!

Another pier collision took place in 1921, when the schooner *Violette* was blown into it by near hurricane-force winds. The collision took place some 200 yards from the old pierhead, and the ship was wedged amongst broken piles and timbers. The crew of eight, under Captain Knott, were all on board at the time and had to scramble up the pier to safety.

The ship weighed 162 tons and was bound for London (from Antwerp) with a general cargo of steel girders and logs. It crashed into the pier at full-speed, 'it being impossible to sail her against the gale', and damaged 150 feet of the structure.

The storm which claimed the *Violette* also brought havoc to other parts of the county, causing structural damage at Kelvedon and Danbury and toppling a tree onto tram wires at London Road, Chalkwell.

In modern times there have also been shipwrecks off the Essex coast. One was the 1982 *European Gateway* ferry disaster, which happened within sight of Harwich. At around 11pm on Sunday 19 December it collided with another ship, the *Speedlink Vanguard*, and turned over onto its side where it rested on a sandbank. Other ships in the area quickly came to the rescue and managed to take off most of the people on board. Several people died in this disaster, caused by human error.

In 1986 the *Kingsabbey* became the latest ship to collide with Southend Pier. The following year's 'hurricane' in October overturned several vessels, including some that were 'safely' in harbour.

Ship design continues to improve, and chances of shipwrecks should therefore reduce, but in a maritime county, safety from the sea can never be guaranteed.

CHAPTER X

Air Disasters

Early aviators found out with difficulty that getting airborne was no mean achievement, but imagine the sense of fulfilment felt by such pioneers as the Wright brothers when their home-made contraptions eventually got off the ground.

Air travel has developed greatly since the first decade of the 20th century, but things can still go wrong. Television pictures of air disasters such as those at Tenerife, Schipol (Amsterdam) and Lockerbie have brought home to all the horrors of such incidents in recent years. From the balloons of early aviators to modern air incidents, this chapter provides a selection of some of the more hair-raising aerial exploits which have taken place in Essex.

Before aeroplanes were invented, ballooning was the most popular form of air travel. Famous

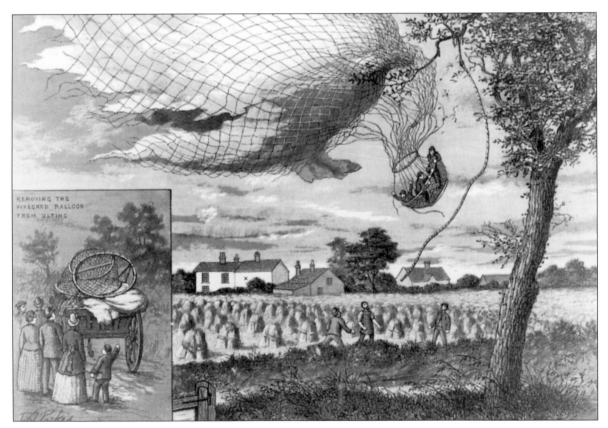

125 The Ulting balloon accident of 1888, showing the house (marked with a 'X') where the dying Joseph Simmons was taken.

balloonists like Joseph Simmons were highly regarded as brave and dashing 'aeronauts'. Unfortunately, however, things did not always go to plan.

Simmons had made nearly 500 balloon flights over a period of almost 30 years when he left Olympia in London with two colleagues, Mr. Field and Mr. Miers, on Monday, 27 August 1888. Their plan was to fly to Vienna, but it became clear that the wind was in the wrong direction and they drifted instead over Essex, following approximately the line of the London-Colchester railway.

In late afternoon they reached the village of Ulting, 37 miles from Olympia, and Simmons advised his colleagues to land there, rather than risk crossing the North Sea in the dark.

However, the fields around Ulting did not offer a safe landing. Trees were everywhere and it was difficult to see a good place to touch down. Eventually, Simmons selected a field owned by George Wood, the local blacksmith, and threw out the grapnel—an anchor-like hook which was supposed to fix into the ground. Unfortunately, the grapnel fell into a cornfield and failed to grip as it was dragged along by the balloon. As the aeronauts threw out some sandbags to gain height and clear some advancing trees, the grapnel caught in one of the trees and jerked the balloon suddenly to the ground. Simmons shouted to some labourers in a nearby field for assistance, but the balloon basket, a metal cage, crashed hard into the ground and then suddenly rose again, before the balloon burst and the whole ensemble again crashed to the ground.

All three occupants were knocked unconscious. Mr. Field had a broken leg and internal pain, Mr. Miers a cut forehead and two black eyes, but Simmons himself never regained consciousness. He was taken to a local beerhouse run by Mr. Turner where Dr. Gutteridge from Maldon tried his best to revive him. The doctor's efforts were unsuccessful and Simmons died in a coma just before 9pm.

The loss of Joseph Simmons was a major blow to ballooning. It also alerted Essex people to the dangers of air travel even for experienced flyers.

Early aeroplane pilots were not much safer than the pioneers of ballooning. On Tuesday, 3 February 1914 a Royal Naval Flying Corps airman from

126 The Leigh-on-Sea aircrash of February 1914, which fortunately resulted in no injury to the pilot. The coastguard (in the hat, second right) and the local policeman both came to inspect the damage.

127 A propeller memorial to Captain A.B. Kynock and Captain H.C. Stroud, marking the spot where their aircraft fell after they collided over Shotgate, Wickford, on 7 March 1918. The inscription reads: 'This spot is sacred to the memory of Captain H. Clifford Stroud killed in action at midnight on 7 March 1918. Faithful unto Death.'.

occurred. The aeroplane was taken into the care of the Leigh coastguard.

Four years later another air disaster took place in south-east Essex, when on 7 March 1918 two wartime planes collided above Shotgate near Wickford and crashed helplessly to the ground. Both pilots—Captain A.B. Kynock and Captain Henry Clifford Stroud—were killed, and there is a memorial at the spot in a field where one of the planes fell. Captain Stroud was buried at Rochford church, whilst Captain Kynock's body was removed for burial to Golders Green.

After the Second World War, the incidents continued. At 3.30pm on Monday, 10 September 1951 an RAF Meteor Jet exploded in mid-air over Westcliff-on-Sea and crashed into houses in Ramuz Drive and Hainault Avenue. Four people were killed including the pilot, who was himself a local man. Parts of the jet landed in streets around the area, causing damage to property and embedding themselves in back-gardens. A passing district nurse was fortunately on hand to help the injured, before continuing her duties elsewhere in the town.

Most of the damage, and the three civilian deaths, occurred in Ramuz Drive. Beedell Avenue, Brightwell Avenue and Inverness Avenue were other local streets affected. The accident was a horrifying reminder of the aerial attacks during the Second World War and the local paper, *The Southend Standard*, was quick to call for a review of flying operations. 'The changing tempo of modern flying,' ran the paper's editorial, 'demands a revision of the regulations governing the flight of aircraft over built-up areas.'

The dead pilot was buried near his airbase at Wattisham in Suffolk. A scheduled Battle of Britain memorial service at St Michael's Church in Westcliff provided an additional occasion for those killed in the disaster to be remembered.

Since the 1950s the number of flights in and out of Essex airports has continued to increase, but the county retains a good air safety record. London Stansted and London Southend Airports are both integral parts of Britain's transport network, whilst other aerodromes, such as Stapleford Abbotts, provide local facilities for flying enthusiasts.

Eastchurch was forced to land his Bristol biplane in a field between Leigh-on-Sea and Hadleigh, when he ran out of lubricating oil. His colleague, Sub-Lieutenant Rainey, was dispatched to assist him, but soon got into difficulties himself.

The first plane was topped up with oil and took off safely but, when Rainey took off, his plane reached a height of only 60 feet before one of the wings collapsed and the plane came crashing to the ground. Fortunately the airman only suffered shock and bruises and he spent the night with a local doctor who happened to be passing when the crash

128 The fuselage of a crashed RAF Meteor jet in Hainault Avenue, Westcliff-on-Sea, following its mid-air explosion in September 1951.

CHAPTER XI

Special Occasions

The previous chapters have covered some of the more disastrous events. Amongst more pleasant events, Essex has hosted numerous visits by famous people—members of the Royal family, MPs and popstars. Such events always prove popular with ordinary people and visits by dignitaries to the county have often gone down in Essex folklore.

There have been many historic Royal visits to the county. Richard II came to Pleshey in 1397, Henry VII was at Hedingham a century later and Henry VIII was at New Hall, Boreham,

on several occasions. His daughters, Mary I and Elizabeth I, also visited New Hall, whilst Elizabeth virtually invented the formal 'Royal visit' with her many county 'Progresses'. From Loughton to Harwich, Saffron Walden to Maldon, she travelled extensively around the county. In 1561 she was entertained at Ingatestone by Sir William Petre and may well have returned there in 1579. Her most famous visit was in 1588 when she journeyed to Tilbury, where she reviewed the troops preparing for the invasion of

129 A picture from *c.*1915 showing the 'Queen's Oak' (centre)—a tree planted on behalf of Queen Victoria to commemorate her visit to High Beach in 1882 formally to open Epping Forest to the public. The tree on the left is the now-vanished King's Oak, said to have been planted by King Harold.

the Spanish Armada and greatly encouraged them with a memorable speech.

James I visited the massive mansion at Audley End near Saffron Walden a decade after Elizabeth's death and Charles I and his mother-in-law, Mary Medici, visited Chelmsford and several other places in south Essex in 1638. The 17th-century diarists, John Evelyn and Samuel Pepys, also travelled local roads, whilst the writer, Daniel Defoe, was a notable visitor in the 1720s.

In 1778 George III visited Thorndon Hall near Brentwood and then went to Warley to review the troops. At Thorndon he was the guest of the 9th Lord Petre, whose elaborate preparations for the King's arrival are recorded in his highly entertaining diary. Up to 100 servants were employed in the fortnight before the visit to ensure that nothing went wrong with the preparations. On the day of the King's arrival, the park was full of artillery firing off salutes and the King was accompanied by a huge train of provisions and attendants.

One of the most celebrated visits to Essex by a reigning monarch was by Queen Victoria to High Beach on Saturday, 6 May 1882 to declare Epping Forest open to the public. This marked a significant change in forest policy and was the result of a long campaign by the Corporation of the City of London to end the (usually illegal) practice whereby local landowners enclosed parts of the forest for themselves.

A local man, Thomas Willingale, sparked off the campaign by insisting on his traditional rights to lop forest trees even where they stood on enclosed land. A court case was brought against him but he, his sons and friends steadfastly stood by their rights and refused to be quietened by angry landowners. When Willingale died the Corporation took up the cudgels and continued to press for freedom of access to the forest. Their campaign culminated in the 1878 Epping Forest Act, which legally invested the Corporation as the Forest's Conservators, effectively giving them ownership and responsibility for its 6,000 acres.

Four years later a spectacular celebration took place and Queen Victoria arrived at a specially built marquee in High Beach formally to declare the Forest open to the public. 'It gives me the greatest satisfaction,' she told a huge crowd of commoners and dignitaries, 'to dedicate this beautiful forest to the use and enjoyment of my people for all time.'

The Queen arrived at High Beach via a carriage procession from Chingford station, where a reception room had been decorated in the finest materials—silk, satin and ivory amongst them—and where huge crowds were waiting to meet her from the train. Half a million people are thought to have turned up for the occasion, most travelling from the East End of London. 'Four-in-hands and private carriages with liveried servants rubbed wheels with omnibuses, wagonettes, picnic vans and with the still humbler coster's barrow', wrote a contemporary newspaper reporter, whom the whole procession reminded 'of Epsom on Derby-Day.'

Since Victoria's visit to Epping Forest there have been countless visits by other dignitaries to open other facilities and institutions in Essex. In October 1892, for example, Castle Park in Colchester was officially opened by the Lord Mayor of London.

On Saturday, 3 February 1906 Lady Rayleigh opened a new library, museum and arts centre at Chelmsford. The building had been designed by the Mayor, Frederick Chancellor, and Mr. Wykeham Chancellor, and was a long-awaited facility for the town. According to contemporary newspaper reports it was too small, but it had been designed to enable easily added extensions if the demand was there.

130 The procession accompanying Lady Rayleigh to open the Free Library at Chelmsford on Saturday, 3 February 1906.

131 The flagship of the Home & Atlantic Fleets, the battleship *Dreadnought*—one of a group of 149 ships which visited Southend in July 1909. The ship weighed 17,900 tons, was 490 feet in length and cost £2 million to build. The 'submarine attack' of the caption was probably a simulated exercise as part of the celebrations.

132 Part of the parade marking the arrival of the Lord Mayor of London to Southend-on-Sea, when the Home and Atlantic Fleets visited the town in July 1909.

133 The visit of the Russian Duma to inspect the troops at Colchester on 11 May 1916.

Lady Rayleigh performed the opening ceremony by turning a silver key in the lock of the front door and was then taken on a tour where she viewed a full set of *Encyclopaedia Britannica,* the *Century Dictionary* and *Allen's Naturalists' Library*, as well as some museum exhibits loaned by the South Kensington Natural History Museum. Lord Rayleigh laid the foundation stone several months earlier, so it was fitting for Lady Rayleigh to perform the official opening. The building cost £8,000 to construct, financed in part by a £2,500 donation from the well-known philanthropist, Andrew Carnegie.

Apart from the visits of individuals to Essex, there have also been some large-scale visits by groups.

In July 1909 the residents of Southend-on-Sea were treated to an impressive spectacle when 149 ships from the British Home and Atlantic Fleets and accompanying Cruiser Squadron anchored in the River Thames as part of an exercise to boost publicity for the town and give the Admiralty publicity for further warship building.

The Fleet, under Commander-in-Chief Admiral Sir W.H. May in his flagship battleship *Dreadnought*, began arriving in the Thames on Wednesday 14 July and stayed until Saturday 24 July. Southend's seafront, High Street and environs were bedecked with hundreds of banners, flags and Chinese lanterns to welcome the 42,000 sailors who crewed the 24 battleships, 16 armoured cruisers, 19 protective cruisers and auxiliary ships, 48 destroyers, 6 torpedo boats, 34 submarines and 2 repair ships of the visiting Fleet.

The Lord Mayor of London and the Lords Commissioners of the Admiralty were present during 'Fleet Week', with local dignitaries such as Southend's Mayor, Alderman Ingram. Special dinners for the sailors were provided in both Southend and London and townspeople were given the opportunity to look round some of the ships.

The vessels were arranged in rows stretching from Leigh-on-Sea to the Nore. On the evening of Thursday, 22 July they were all illuminated—an incredible sight witnessed by an estimated 250,000 people! The whole event captured the public's imagination, and cartoons, poems and souvenir pictures appeared in the local press. A souvenir booklet was also issued to commemorate the occasion and some of the sailors were given their own mementoes of the visits to Southend and London. Local tradesmen estimated their combined takings for the week at over £100,000!

The exercise was considered, not surprisingly, to be a resounding success. The local newspaper, The *Southend & Westcliff Graphic*, described it as 'the most wonderful armada the world has ever seen … which makes the British Empire the foremost in the world'.

Seven years later, on 11 May 1916, members of the Russian Duma—that country's parliament—went to Colchester. It was not their first visit to the town, as they had been present at a Historical Pageant there in 1909.

The purpose of their visit on this occasion was to inspect the troops at Colchester barracks and they were met at Marks Tey railway station by the town's mayor and fellow councillors, as well as by Essex's Chief Constable and various army staff. After stopping at Stanway for a troop inspection, they were taken by car to a second inspection at Colchester's Abbey Field. The Town Council laid on a luncheon and then took the visitors on a tour of historical places in the locality.

The Vice-President of the Duma 'expressed admiration at the wonderful review he and his colleagues had witnessed and said the magnificent army which England had raised since the commencement of the war was typical of British energy in trade and commerce'.

After the First World War a section of the Home and Atlantic Fleets returned to Southend-on-Sea to help the town commemorate the national Peace Celebrations of July 1919. The visit was on a smaller scale than that of ten years earlier but it once again created a buzz of interest.

Plans to invite the King for the occasion never materialised, but the Lord Mayor of London inspected the 20-odd battleships and cruisers and the accompanying destroyer and submarine flotillas. Southend's Mayor, Alderman F.W. Senier, entertained many of the men and officers at special events in the town and many more were made welcome at local sports clubs, swimming and yachting matches and other community events.

The Fleet visit officially lasted from 17-23 July, though some ships started arriving a couple of days beforehand. The flagship, *Queen Elizabeth*, and Commander-in-Chief Admiral Sir Charles Madden, played host to visitors from Southend Corporation, whilst members of the public were treated to visits to some of the other ships.

Local entertainments for the week included Navy bands playing at the Cliffs bandstand, a spectacular choreographed searchlight display and, on the evening of Saturday, 19 July (Peace Day), the complete illumination of the Fleet.

The *Southend Standard* issued a special 'Fleet Visit Supplement', containing photographs of the ships and details of various related events in the town.

134 The illuminated fleet at Southend-on-Sea on Saturday, 19 July 1919. The ships were illuminated as part of a national 'Peace Day', marking the end of the First World War.

135 The Duke of York unveiling a fountain at Priory Park, Prittlewell on 14 July 1920.

'With Southend and District,' recorded the paper's editorial the day after the ships had left, 'Peace Day will ever be remembered in connection with the visit of the Fleet, and those who had the opportunity of witnessing the illumination of the battleships, destroyers and submarines on Saturday night will not easily have that sight effaced from their memory.'

The following year, Southend townsfolk were treated to another high profile visit, by the Duke of York formally to open Priory Park. The donation of the Prittlewell park in 1917 to the people of Southend was one of many beneficent acts by the well-known local jeweller, R.A. Jones. The official opening was postponed until the First World War was over and 1920 offered the first opportunity for it to take place. The Duke of York, later King George VI, performed the ceremony on 14 July.

A plaque on the main gates records that 'this park, comprising over 30 acres, with its gardens and the mansion called the Priory in which are incorporated some buildings of the Cluniac Priory of St Mary of Prittlewell, was presented by R.A. Jones Esq. to the inhabitants of the County Borough of Southend-on-Sea for perpetual public use A.D. 1917'. The park's fountain also carries an appropriate inscription: 'Presented by R.A. Jones MBE, honorary freeman of Southend-on-Sea, in commemoration of the glorious dead of this Borough who gave their all for Britain in the Great War 1914-1919'.

Twenty years later the north of the county received a Royal visit, when in June 1938 Queen Mary toured several places on the Essex-Suffolk border, including Brightlingsea, Colchester, Flatford Mill (just across the river from Dedham) and St Osyth's Priory. The Brightlingsea visit was the first by a Royal visitor within living memory and generated a lot of interest, with a 'warm vocal welcome and wide display of flags and bunting'. The Queen visited Jacobs (an ancient mansion) and the town's oyster fishermen, who presented her with a 'monster lobster'.

Apart from Royalty, one of the country's greatest statesmen has a direct Essex connection—former Prime Minister Sir Winston Churchill was MP for both Epping and Woodford. He was also a visitor to Frinton as a child and paid an impromptu visit to Clacton just before the First World War when his plane ditched in the sea and he had to put up with some abuse from local suffragettes!

In modern times, Queen Elizabeth II and other members of the Royal family have visited Essex on numerous occasions. In 1953 the Queen was at

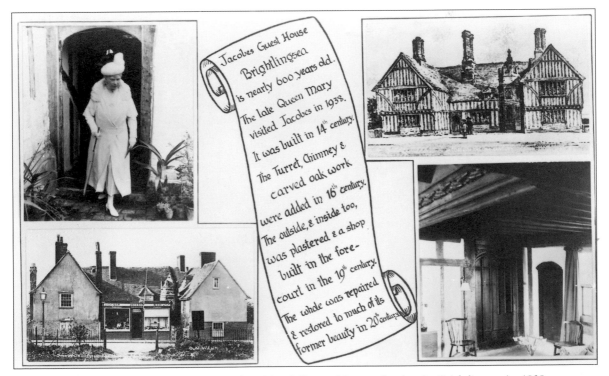

136 A postcard commemorating the visit of Queen Mary to Jacobes in Brightlingsea in 1938.

137   Her Majesty Queen Elizabeth II waves to royal supporters after formally opening the 'Queen Elizabeth II Bridge' in Thurrock on 30 October 1991.

Tilbury in the wake of the 'Great Tide' floods to give moral support. In 1971 she was at Maldon for the 800th-anniversary celebrations of the town's first Royal charter. In 1988 she made one of several visits to Chelmsford and in October 1991 she performed the opening ceremony of the 'Queen Elizabeth II Bridge', which connects Essex to Kent. She unveiled a monument on the Essex side which records the bridge's name and the date of its opening.

The Queen's Golden Jubilee, in the early years of the 21st century, offers a further prospect of Royal and other visits to the county.

As well as celebrations attended by visiting dignitaries, there have been numerous other special occasions to celebrate. Coronations and Royal weddings have always been popular, as have celebrations at the ends of wars. On the other hand, several major funerals have taken place and religious ceremonies and various ceremonial presentations have also attracted large crowds.

In July 1821 the coronation of King George IV was celebrated in Chelmsford with a musical procession around the town and a meal laid out on tables in the High Street, stretching from the now-demolished *Black Boy* at one end to the *Saracen's Head* at the other. There were floral displays throughout the town, a fireworks display was laid on outside the Shire Hall and the revelry continued until dawn the following morning.

Ten years later, in September 1831, similar festivities greeted King William IV's coronation. At Horndon-on-the-Hill there was a good display of fireworks 'and a liberal distribution of ale to the poor'. Three hundred poor people at Rayleigh were given beer, while at Springfield 1,100 tucked into 'a hearty meal' of beef and plum pudding.

In June 1838 Queen Victoria was crowned, the start of a long and memorable reign. Cannon-fire opened the celebrations at Chelmsford—some of it carried out unofficially by 'some rather indiscreet persons' who accidentally broke a few windows at the Shire Hall! In Colchester, the High Street was decorated with green boughs, whilst musical events and school sports in the castle bailey provided entertainment throughout the day. Over 9,000 poor people in the town were each given a pound of beef and a sixpence to mark the occasion.

Victoria's Golden and Diamond Jubilees, in 1887 and 1897 respectively, were also widely celebrated and numerous memorials survive. The clocktower in Coggeshall was raised in height to mark the Golden Jubilee and it still bears the date, 1887.

The county's 1897 celebrations were centred on Chelmsford, but numerous activities took place in other communities. At Althorne the vicar, Rev. H.M. Milligan, preached on the text of 'Perfect Love Casteth Out Fear', which seemed to him 'the very keynote to the marvellous unanimity of feeling among all

138 1902 Empire Day celebrations outside the Technical Schools at Southend-on-Sea.

parties'. At Vange the Sunday services to mark the occasion were 'extremely bright and hearty, and well rendered throughout … The National Anthem was sung at each service with manifest sincerity and enjoyment on the part of the choir and congregation'. A 'handsome oak seat', subscribed for by parishioners, was placed in Woodham Mortimer churchyard.

Victoria's birthday, 24 May, was celebrated after her death as 'Empire Day'—another excuse for a party and revelry. At Southend in 1902 the Technical Schools which were opened that year were the focus of the celebrations.

Edward VII's coronation was postponed to August 1902 from the previous year owing to the king's ill-health in 1901. The mayors of Chelmsford, Colchester, Maldon, Southend-on-Sea and West Ham were all in attendance at Westminster Abbey, whilst towns throughout the county celebrated with processions and feasts. A 21-gun salute was fired at Braintree. Nearby Dunmow hosted extensive sporting activities.

Three years later, a much sadder occasion was marked in south-west Essex: the funeral procession at Barkingside of Dr. Thomas John Barnardo, who died on 19 September 1905.

Barnardo was a native of Dublin (his father was of Spanish ancestry), who moved to London in 1866 to train as a medical missionary. There he became a pioneer of social work by initially becoming superintendent of an East End school and later by founding homes for poor and destitute children. He founded

139 The funeral procession of Dr. Barnardo at Barkingside in September 1905.

140 The announcement by the High Sheriff of Essex of the accession of King George V on 9 May 1910 in front of the Shire Hall at Chelmsford. The cannon in the background is now in the grounds of the Chelmsford & Essex Museum.

141 King George V's Coronation Bonfire at Eve's Corner, Danbury, on 22 June 1911.

over 90 homes, beginning in 1870 with a boys' home in Stepney and later introducing girls' homes and a 'children's village' in Barkingside. He is said to have helped at least 250,000 children and there is a statue to his memory in the grounds of the Barkingside estate. The design of the statue includes children looking up to the good doctor and features the touching inscription, 'We love him, because he loved us'.

In 1910 there was another royal moment to celebrate: the accession on 9 May of King George V. At Chelmsford, in front of the Shire Hall, the announcement was made by the High Sheriff of Essex. A large crowd gathered to hear the news. The celebrations for George V's coronation in June 1911 were also centred on Chelmsford and virtually every town and village in the county also marked the occasion. At Danbury a coronation committee, under the chairmanship of Colonel F.F. Johnson CB, arranged a day of events, starting at 10am with a service at the parish church. This was followed by a dinner at Danbury Park for everyone over 14 years of age, an afternoon tea for those under 14 and a 'bran tub' for those under six. Sporting events

142 Market Hill, Coggeshall, on Sunday 26 July 1913, showing a Territorial Parade and the presentation of a long-service medal to Joseph Sexton. The picture shows the blue full dress uniform worn by the 8th (Cyclist) Battalion in preference to the usual scarlet and white of the Essex Regiment, which easily became dirty when cycling. In July 1914 the 8th Battalion had 54 members.

and brass band entertainment took place throughout the afternoon and the day ended at 10pm with a bonfire at Eve's Corner.

Coronation honours in the county included Sir John Bethell, MP for Romford Division, who was made a baronet.

In addition to many major national celebrations, there have also been numerous local ones, too. On Sunday, 26 July 1913 in Market Hill, Coggeshall, a Territorial Parade took place and a long-service medal was presented to Joseph Sexton of 'H' Company of the 8th (Cyclist) Battalion, Essex Regiment, Coggeshall's own company. Sexton was a well-known local figure, for several years landlord of the *Chapel Inn*. Another Sexton, R.W., was with the 5th Essex at the same time.

During the First World War, there were many more medal presentations across the county. One of the most poignant was the posthumous award of the Victoria Cross to the former East Ham schoolboy, Jack Cornwell, who was killed at the Battle of Jutland—the First World War's only major sea battle between the British and German fleets. He remained at his post despite serious injury and received the award for his bravery in the face of enemy action. His former school in East Ham was later renamed after him and the children there contributed to a monument which still stands in Manor Park cemetery.

After the War, towns and villages put up memorials to those of their number who had been killed during the conflict. Most memorials were built in the early 1920s and the whole village usually turned out to commemorate those who had fought for their countrymen's freedom and futures.

The Silver Jubilee of King George V in 1935 was an occasion for widespread celebration throughout the county. The *Essex Chronicle* reported that 'the Clerk of the Weather seemed to join in specially, for he provided the most glorious day of the year'.

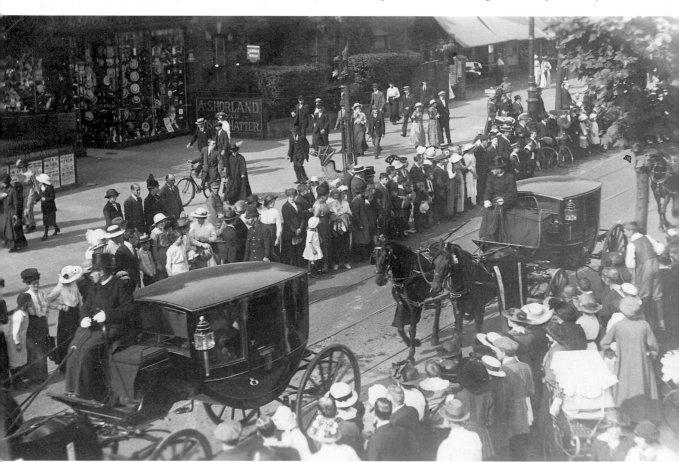

143 The funeral procession at Manor Park, East Ham, of 16-year-old Jack Cornwell VC, who was killed at the Battle of Jutland in 1916.

144   The unveiling of the war memorial at Manuden on 25 September 1921.

145   The war memorial at Southend-on-Sea, unveiled by Lord Lambourne on 27 November 1921. An estimated 20,000 people attended the ceremony and continued to lay wreaths until well after dark. The memorial was designed by the well-known architect and artist, Sir Edwin Lutyens (designer of The Cenotaph in London), and was erected (in the words of the local paper) as 'a tribute… raised in humble thankfulness to those who fell by those who live'.

146 A carnival float from the procession marking the Silver Jubilee celebrations of King George V at Hadleigh in 1935. This was one of two floats entered by the Salvation Army Farm Colony, which owned a vast tract of land in the village. The theme of the float was 'Brickmaking Today', brickmaking being one of the many activities practised at the Colony.

A chain of beacons was lit across the country at night and Chelmsford Cathedral hosted a thanksgiving service. The Lord Lieutenant of Essex joined in this, before attending his own local service at Waltham Abbey.

'The County Town was gaily beflagged in every street,' wrote an *Essex Chronicle* reporter, 'and the principal buildings were illuminated. Coloured festoons adorned the Shire Hall and flags fluttered down from the windows.'

At Braintree the market place was similarly decorated 'with Venetian Masts and streamers' and church bells were rung periodically throughout the day. At Hadleigh a carnival procession took place, with the Salvation Army Farm Colony entering two floats representing Colony activities.

Two years later the Coronation of Edward VIII was not so fortunate with the weather, but again local people turned out for the event. At Ingatestone a 'public tea' was held and trees were planted in the recreation ground.

After the Second World War the VE Day celebrations and parties were perhaps the most enthusiastic for some time, as everyone could relax after many years of war. Victory parties took place all over the county with street parties and sports for the children and, at last, a period of relaxation for the adults.

In the years immediately following the Second World War the Diocesan Youth Council in Essex organised an annual Youth Pilgrimage, which brought together young people from all over the county. During the 1950 pilgrimage 1,200 youngsters took part in a Procession of Witness along the High Street, Moulsham Street, The Friars and London Road, Chelmsford, carrying religious banners and singing hymns such as 'Onward Christian Soldiers' and 'Stand Up, Stand Up For Jesus'. The procession ended at the Cathedral, where the Bishop of Chelmsford led an evening service. Associated events included a play called 'Christmas in the Market Place' by Henri Gheon (presented by Drama Christi and

147 A VE Day party at The Crescent in Hadleigh.

produced by the Reverend Rex Parkin) and a special tea at the Shire Hall and Cathedral Hall. The whole event was described as 'the finest parade of young Christians ever seen in the County Town'.

Three years later the Coronation of Queen Elizabeth II was celebrated all over the county, again despite bad weather. At Southend, local cinemas showed films entitled 'Elizabeth Is Queen' and 'The Coronation', whilst the Darby & Joan fête in Chalkwell Park was memorably opened with appropriate sketches by the comedians Norman Wisdom and Eddie Leslie. An RAF Coronation Ball was held at the Kursaal, with Ted Heath and his music, whilst an open-air cliff-top concert at Westcliff featured singers and musicians clad in duffle-coats to protect them from the rain. The battleship HMS *Vanguard* anchored in the Thames off the town on

the evening of the Coronation produced a display of special illuminations. Schools put on plays about the event and pupils were given souvenirs.

More recently still the silver jubilee of Queen Elizabeth II in 1977 and the weddings of the Prince and Princess of Wales in 1981 and the Duke and Duchess of York in 1986 have been among memorable Royal celebrations. Several Essex towns hosted street parties, whilst the 1977 jubilee also inspired permanent reminders such as local seat unveilings or tree-plantings.

Other celebrations include municipal centenary commemorations for both borough and parish councils, the most recent being the 'Chelmsford 800' celebrations in 1999. In 1992 Southend's Borough Centenary was marked with a fireworks display, old-style costume parade and musical events. One of the

148 A VE Day party in Leigh-on-Sea.

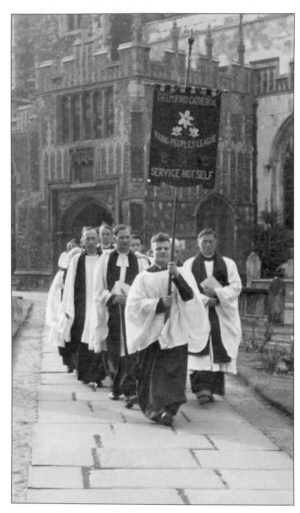

149 The 1950 Youth Pilgrimage at Chelmsford, which took place on Saturday 20 May.

150 The windows of HM Customs & Excise's Alexander House offices, lit up in September 1992 to mark the 100th anniversary of the Borough of Southend.

151 The unveiling on Saturday, 1 February 1997 of a memorial to the 58 Canvey Island residents who lost their lives in the 1953 'Great Tide' flood disaster. The memorial was the idea of local lad, Vincent Heatherson, shown here making a speech at the unveiling ceremony.

town's largest employers, HM Customs & Excise, lit up the windows of 12 floors of its Alexander House office block to spell out '100' on the centenary day in September.

On Saturday, 1 February 1997 a memorial was unveiled to the 58 Canvey residents who lost their lives in the 1953 'Great Tide' flood disaster. The memorial—a commemorative plaque outside Canvey Library, listing the names of those who died in the flooding—was the idea of local lad Vincent Heatherson, who discovered that no memorial had been erected in the 44 years (to the day) since the disaster. The Mayor of Castle Point (the district in which Canvey lies) was present at the unveiling, with over a hundred Canvey residents who paid tribute to those who lost their lives.

The Millennium celebrations for the year 2000 are likely to be as spectacular as any that have gone before.

CHAPTER XII

Miscellaneous

Some events do not conform to any of the previous categories. This chapter examines some of the more unusual activities in Essex, as well as some regular occurrences.

One of the most bizarre events in Essex's history happened in December 1750, when a wager was made between Mr. Codd and Mr. Hants of Maldon: was it possible to fit seven hundred men inside the waistcoat of the recently deceased, larger-than-life local tradesman, Edmund Bright? At his death a month earlier at the age of just 29 Bright weighed over 40 stones and a hole had to be cut in the wall of his house to get his coffin out. The bet was eventually won on the somewhat dubious grounds that the person proposing it had meant 'seven Hundred men', i.e. seven men from Dengie Hundred (the administrative district in which Maldon lay), could be fitted inside the garment!

The Dunmow Flitch Ceremony is well-known in Essex, where couples who have been married for at least a year and a day volunteer to be put on trial to prove their faithfulness to each other, in the hope of gaining a flitch of bacon in reward. Six maidens and six bachelors from Great Dunmow sit in judgement on the competitors and lawyers are appointed to state the case for the appellants and, bizarrely, for the bacon. The winners are carried shoulder high on an ancient chair through the streets of the town and the whole event provides an occasion for extensive merriment and entertainment.

152 An engraving of the day in December 1750 when a bet about fitting 'seven Hundred men' into Edmund Bright's waistcoat was put to the test.

The obscure origins of the Flitch ceremony date from the 12th century, when a flitch of bacon was handed out from the priory at Little Dunmow to any couple who claimed it. Later presentation was carried out by the Lord of the Manor and the practice evidently gained such fame that it was mentioned in one of the earliest works of English Literature, *Piers Plowman*, by William Langland (14th-century).

Over the years the event seemed to have died out. It was reinstated in modern times by the novelist, Harrison Ainsworth (1855), following a well-publicised case four years earlier when a claim for a flitch by a local couple was rejected by the Lord of the Manor. There was huge popular interest following the ceremony's reinstatement and thousands of people attended. Nowadays, it is run every leap year by Dunmow Town Council and there is still much interest

153   A classic engraving of the winners of the Dunmow Flitch Ceremony in 1751, Mr. & Mrs. Shakeshaft. Thousands of people attended that year's event, blocking local roads and partaking in a great deal of merrymaking.

154   A marvellous photograph of what is thought to be the 1920 Dunmow Flitch Ceremony. This was the first such ceremony after the First World War and appears to have generated significant interest—resulting in the production of postcards of the event.

155 A classic picture of Braintree market in 1826.

amongst local townsfolk, potential claimants and the regional media.

More mundane but equally well-supported have been the numerous markets around the county. Essex has several famous market towns, including Romford, Halstead, Braintree and others. The market at Braintree, one of the oldest in the county, is still going strong 800 years after King John issued its charter in 1199. It was anciently situated in Great Square, Bank Street, Swan Side and Drury Lane, but the original stalls were gradually replaced by permanent buildings. It was later moved into Market Place and New Street and in its heyday it sold everything from livestock to farm implements and carpets. It still operates today, on Wednesdays and Saturdays, in Bank Street and Market Place.

Markets provide a source of employment; an unusual scheme in the south west of the county was the hiring of men to enlarge the lakes in Epping Forest. Some lakes there were enlarged solely for the purpose of taking on unemployed people—a commendable, if somewhat unusual, local practice.

Most of this sort of lake enlargement seems to have taken place in the early part of the 20th century.

At the same time, in the south east of the county, an unusual discovery was made in West Street, Prittlewell. In 1906 a house called Reynolds was demolished to make way for an extension to an adjacent public house, the *Blue Boar*. During the demolition work a rare ancient fireplace was discovered and removed, initially, to the Victoria & Albert Museum. It has since been returned to Southend, where it can be seen on display, fully reconstructed, in the town's Central Museum in Victoria Avenue. Some photographs of Reynolds, which was built in the 14th and 15th centuries, are also on display in the museum.

Three years later, in June 1909, a Historical Pageant was staged in the north east of the county, in Colchester castle grounds. It ran from Monday, 21 June to Saturday, 26 and featured mounted cavalcades, spectacular costumes and choral narration that told the history of Colchester from the Druids to the Civil War, from Boadicea's attack on the town to the discovery of Colchester oysters. A grandstand for 7,000 spectators was built and the event was opened by the Lord Mayor of London. Colchester's own Mayor—W. Gurney Benham—played a leading part in the organisation of the pageant and

156 An intriguing photograph of a labouring gang at work in Epping Forest. It is thought that the men are enlarging one of the forest lakes, as the size of the gang pictured is larger than a usual forest workforce and activities such as lake-enlargement often required extra workers to be taken on. Some lakes were actually enlarged solely for the purpose of reducing the numbers of unemployed. The planks are probably there to provide wheel-barrow access—a wheel-barrow can be seen towards the back of the central plank on the right-hand side of the picture. The date of the photograph is unknown.

157 The 15th-century fireplace discovered at West Street, Prittlewell, during the demolition of a house called Reynolds in 1906.

appeared in several scenes. The event was described by the *Essex Chronicle* as a 'great civil and military spectacle' with 'unique and stirring scenes'.

Another Historical Pageant was held at Westcliff-on-Sea in July that year to raise funds for the NSPCC. It featured several scenes based on local history, including the story of Anne Boleyn, whose father owned nearby Rochford Hall.

The following year there was a Children's Pageant in Ilford, featuring over 1,000 local children, many from Dr. Barnardo's Homes. Scenes in the pageant were based on Essex history, including 'Will Kemp's Dance', 'The Ilford Leper Hospital' and 'The Royal Progress of Queen Elizabeth'. At the same time an 'Orient Exhibition' was held, including such attractions as a 'New Guinea girl'.

Sports events have been popular throughout Essex history. One of the most interesting was the Long Road motorcycle speed trial at Dedham in summer 1913. Rudge, Triumph and Zenith-Gradua machines all took part—a flying-start, half-mile sprint with Tourist Trophy and 1,000cc classes. Mark Head, on a TT-type Zenith-Gradua, appears to have won most of the trophies!

Eight years later the town of Thaxted had an impromptu competition of its own, when it was

158 The Colchester Historical Pageant of 1909, depicting Catherine of Aragon and her entourage on a pilgrimage to Walsingham. The town's mayor, W. Gurney Benham, took part in several scenes, including this one (centre).

159   A scene from the Historical Pageant at Westcliff-on-Sea in July 1909.

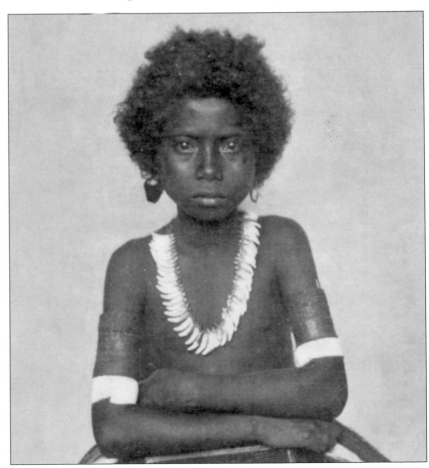

160 A New Guinea girl at
The Orient Exhibition, taken
from a postcard simultaneously
advertising the Ilford Children's
Pageant of June 1910.

161 Competitors in a motorcycle race at Long Road, Dedham in 1913.

162 The Red Flag in Thaxted Church in 1921—part of the infamous 'Battle of the Flags' episode which was sparked by the strongly socialist vicar, Conrad Noel.

163 The skeleton of a witch discovered at St Osyth in 1921.

shaken by a strange local scandal known as the 'Battle of the Flags'. The strongly socialist vicar, Conrad Noel, had hung the Red Flag (and several others) in his church during the First World War and it had survived there relatively peacefully until 1921 when it was unexpectedly removed by persons unknown. Noel replaced it, but it was taken down for a second time, this time by students from Cambridge University. Undaunted, the vicar replaced it again, but the incident attracted sufficient attention to the siting of the flag in church that it became controversial. The hanging of the flag there was not universally popular and the Reverend Noel was ordered by a Church committee to remove it.

In the same year the skeletons of two witches were discovered in Mill Street, St Osyth, by a local man digging in his garden. The bones of the

skeletons were held together by iron spikes, linking the main joints (elbow to elbow, wrist to wrist, etc.), apparently to stop the witches escaping from their graves. The skeletons were thought to be women convicted during the prolific Essex witch hunts of the mid-17th century—one may well have been that of Ursula Kemp, who was said to have put spells on several of her neighbours.

The story of 17th-century witchcraft in Essex demands a book to itself; the discovery of the skeleton of Ursula Kemp is just one of many remarkable events recorded in the county—from the 1884 earthquake to the 1921 'Battle of the Flags', from the 991 Battle of Maldon to the 1991 opening of the Queen Elizabeth II Bridge. The future will surely produce many more to add to the continuing succession of 'Essex Events'.

Select Bibliography

Bowyer, Michael J.F., *Air Raid!* (1986)
Cassidy, Raymond, *Copped Hall —A Short History* (1994)
Corporation of London, *The Official Guide to Epping Forest* (1993)
Currie, Ian, Davison, Mark, and Ogley, Bob, *The Essex Weather Book* (1992)
Dictionary of National Biography
Earnshaw, Alan, *Trains in Trouble* (1996)
Earthquake In Essex (1974)
Edwards, A.C., *A History of Essex* (1994)
Essex Chronicle (various issues)
Essex Countryside (various issues)
Essex Record Office, *Essex at War 1939-45* (1995)
Furbank, Kevan and King, Tom, *History As It Happened* (1990)
Graphic, The (various issues)
Grieve, Hilda, *The Great Tide* (1959)
Gyford, Janet, *Men of Bad Character—the Witham Fires of the 1820s* (1991)
Haining, Peter, *The Great English Earthquake* (1976)
Hall, Peter, *Wickford* (1996)
Harland, M.G. and H.J., *The Flooding of Eastern England* (1980)
Hussey, Stephen, and Swash, Lorna, *'Horrid Lights'—19th-century Incendiarism in Essex* (1994)
Ilford Guardian (various issues)
Ilford Recorder (various issues)
Illustrated London News (various issues)
Jarvis, Stan, *Essex Headlines* (1991)
Jarvis, Stan, *Essex Murder Casebook* (1994)
Jarvis, Stan, *Victorian & Edwardian Essex* (1973)
Kelly's Directory (various editions)
King, Tom, and Furbank, Kevan, *The Southend Story—A Town And Its People* (1991)
Livesey, Anthony, *Atlas of World War I* (1994)
Marriage, John, *Braintree & Bocking—A Pictorial History* (1994)
Mee, Arthur, *The King's England—Essex* (1942)
Payne, Jessie K., *Southend-on-Sea—A Pictorial History* (1985)
Putterill, Jack, *Conrad Noel—Prophet & Priest* (1962)
Romford Times (various issues)
Scollan, Maureen, *Sworn to Serve* (1993)
Southend & Westcliff Graphic (various issues)
Southend Standard (various issues)
Wakeling, Alf, *Brightlingsea, Memorable Occasions* (1986)
Weaver, Leonard T., *The Harwich Story* (1975)
Wright, C.E., *The Fate of Zeppelin L32* (1990) [reprint]
Yearsley, Ian, *Dedham, Flatford & East Bergholt—A Pictorial History* (1996)
Yearsley, Ian, *Hadleigh Past* (1998)
Yearsley, Ian, *Ingatestone & Fryerning—A History* (1997)
Yearsley, Ian, *Islands of Essex* (1994)

Index

References which relate to illustrations are given in **bold**.